The *Columbia* is Coming!

Doris Andersen

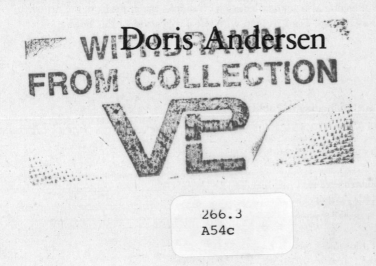

go GRAY'S PUBLISHING LTD.
SIDNEY, B.C., CANADA

Copyright © 1982 by Doris Andersen

Cover by Edward R. Turner, Pender Island, B.C.
Typesetting by The Typeworks, Mayne Island, B.C.

Gray's Publishing acknowledges with thanks the grant from the Anglican
Foundation to assist in the publication of *The Columbia is Coming!*

Gray's Publishing also acknowledges with thanks the grant from the British
Columbia Heritage Trust to help with the publication of this book.

Canadian Cataloguing in Publication Data

Andersen, Doris, 1909–
     The Columbia is coming!

     Bibliography: p.
     Includes index.
     ISBN 0–88826–094–6

     1. Columbia Coast Mission. 2. Anglican
Church of Canada—Missions. 3.– Missions—
British Columbia—History. 4. Boats and
boating in missionary work—British Columbia.
I. Title.
BV2815.B7A53   266'.3711   c81–091289–9

For Lettice

Contents

Acknowledgements

The author is especially grateful to the reference departments of the Vancouver Public Library and University of British Columbia; to Mr. Garth Walker, archivist, and his assistant Mr. Collison of the Vancouver School of Theology, and the former archivist, the Reverend Canon Williams; to archivist Kent Haworth of the Provincial Archives in Victoria; to the Anglican Synod office in Victoria; to children of the first two superintendents of the Columbia Coast Mission (Mr. Ernest Antle, Mrs. F. Mennis, Mr. Alan Greene, Mrs. Catherine Greene Tuck) and the many doctors, clergymen, loggers, settlers and crews of the ships who supplied information, anecdotes and photographs. A partial list appears under Sources.

My sincere thanks also to my editor, Maralyn Horsdal, who persuaded me to undertake the work, and whose encouragement and advice were invaluable.

An Explorations grant from the Canada Council to aid in research, and from the Anglican Foundation to aid in publication are acknowledged with gratitude.

Due to the frequent changeover in staff of crew, clergy and doctors during the 64 years of the Columbia Coast Mission's fleet (some served for very brief periods), the author regrets that limited space has prevented the inclusion of many who contributed to the great work of the mission ships.

Chapter One

Beginnings

I

Early in December 1929, the graceful hospital ship *Columbia* threaded her way among the many islands, large and small, that cluster along the northern shores of Queen Charlotte Strait. She was on her regular route, covering over 10,000 miles, visiting some 89 isolated camps, cabins, lighthouses and floating homes from Seymour Inlet to Rock Bay. The sick were treated, messages of settlers or loggers were carried from one stop to another, and magazines and books were dropped off for news-hungry pioneers.

With Captain Ed Godfrey at the wheel, the *Columbia* came down from Kingcome Inlet and was opposite the entrance to Greenway Sound when the captain's eye was caught by a moving speck that rose and fell on the waves. Changing course, he sailed closer until the speck became a small boat with a boy about 15 standing up as he rowed, and stopping at intervals to wave his shirt in a frantic signal of distress. He was a big, husky youth, but when the *Columbia* reached him he had collapsed on the seat, head bowed, sobbing with relief.

"Oh boy, it was good to see you stop and change course," he told the crew as they helped him aboard. "A man's hurt bad, down at our camp."

"Lucky you got out here when you did," they said. "Ten minutes later we'd have been in the sound, headed north for Bull Harbour."

The *Columbia* took the rowboat in tow and followed the boy's directions to a small camp half an hour's run away. The little camp was not on the ship's agenda; it had been set up only a short time and its existence was unknown to the crew. They tied up to a log boom in front of the shack and the boy led the four crew members up a steep incline and along a rough logging trail. Besides Godfrey, the *Columbia*'s crew included Dr. Herschel Stringer, Cecil Fitzgerald the engineer, and Tony Katsumato, cook.

Three loggers, Glassford, Jackson and young Jones, had been logging in the Simoom Sound area, felling the trees by hand and dragging them with a team of horses to a chute that ran the logs down to the beach. John Glassford had taken the horses that morning to collect firewood to use during the coming Christmas season so the crew could relax and be comfortably warm over the holiday.

As he led the team across a log bridge over a ravine, the big, heavy horses crashed through the flooring and man and animals fell into the deep gully, landing at the bottom pinioned beneath the logs. One horse was killed instantly. The other was positioned so that its hoofs were opposite the man's head and chest as it struggled to free itself. Glassford was kicked again and again by the flying hoofs of the dying animal.

He lay in agony for hours before his partners set out to look for him. They got the logs off him but his injuries were terrible and they dared not move him. Young Jones was told to take the rowboat and try to locate the hospital ship *Columbia* which might be somewhere in the area. Desperately the boy had rowed among those uninhabited islands, straining his eyes for the sight of a ship, hoping against hope that his signal would be seen.

When the *Columbia*'s crew reached the ravine, Dr. Stringer gave emergency treatment, the injured man was lifted to a stretcher and the slow procession to the ship began. It took

2

them over an hour to cover the long trail, and the difficult descent down the incline to the beach was made doubly awkward with the bulky stretcher. At Alert Bay hospital, Glassford was found by Dr. C.A. Watson to have broken ribs, broken legs, one broken arm and the other arm badly damaged, a bad cut on his forehead and one eye almost kicked out by the horse's hoofs. Yet he recovered eventually, due in large part to the crew of the *Columbia* and the staff of the mission hospital.[1]

Later that year, the *Columbia* made her annual two-week Christmas tour to entertain children at some 25 of her regular stops. Superintendent John Antle had come from Vancouver to take over the ship while Captain Godfrey was on leave. The hospital of the *Columbia* was piled high with toys as she turned in at Echo Bay, sounding bell and whistle to herald her coming. Here there was a floating village composed of several little houses erected on one big raft. These floating homes were found along the coast in bays and up the inlets and were owned mainly by loggers with small outfits who logged close to the water and moved their rafts about from one logging area to another. Some consisted of only one little shack; some were like a tiny village with a store to supply their needs. At Echo Bay, children attended a one-room school across the bay, ferrying themselves over the water on a small raft by pulling, hand over hand, along an overhead line.

The boat's whistle had brought children tumbling from the cabins. Parents followed, lines were secured to the logs and the entire population of the floating village crowded aboard to see the decorated tree that stood in a corner of the ship's cabin, securely fastened to withstand the buffeting of stormy winter seas. The *Columbia*'s young Irish engineer, Cecil Fitzgerald, set up screen and projector, and shrieks of laughter greeted the antics of Charlie Chaplin and Felix the Cat. Most of the children were seeing their first movie. Fitzgerald slipped away and reappeared, disguised with white beard and whiskers and red Santa suit, to hand out toys. When the excitement died down, John Antle held a brief service. These Christmas visits of the beautiful *Columbia* were highlights in the lives of logging and pioneering families in isolated bays and up the long, lonely inlets on Vancouver Island and the mainland.

Weddings held on the ships were a popular choice; they offered a unique setting, and most camps were a long distance from stationary churches. The ship's chaplain was always willing to oblige, though services were sometimes speeded up if an emergency call came in. Christenings, marriages and funerals were held on board. One logger's wedding was held in the cabin of the ambulance ship *Rendezvous*. As the wedding party approached in a rowboat, chaplain Greene piped them aboard with the ship's little portable organ. The bride changed from hobnailed boots to satin slippers before entering the ship's cabin but donned the boots again to go ashore for the reception, where she cut the cake, appropriately enough, with a double-bitted axe.

In 1905, the year that saw the start of the Columbia Coast Mission's marine fleet, Vancouver Island and the islands and mainland coast adjacent to it were dotted with small logging camps and canneries. Men from as far away as Québec, the United States, and European and Asiatic countries found their way to British Columbia in search of the good life they had yet to discover. Some had the goldfields of the north as their original objective, but when funds ran out they settled for work in the coastal logging camps or canneries. Misfits and alcoholics unable or unwilling to hold permanent jobs also drifted to the irregular work in these areas. Many workers brought families with them, and when logging outfits completed their show and moved out, they sought work in other camps or threw up little shacks on the banks of inlets and turned to handlogging and fishing in an effort to make ends meet.

Logging accidents were frequent and often fatal, but no medical service or first-aid equipment was available in the camps. There were no hospitals in the vast area between Bella Bella and Victoria[2], and transportation to such points was by slow coastal steamers that made numerous stops to load and unload freight on their leisurely trips. These neglected loggers and settlers were the people that John Antle set out to serve with hospitals and ambulance ships for the sick and injured, and social and spiritual aid to all those in this isolated area. Through the Depression era the mission ships were a vital force in aiding distressed and needy families.

Over the years, large logging companies and canneries gradually absorbed the smaller concerns and many outfits on the marine mission's calling list ceased to exist. Planes took over the transportation for emergencies, and by 1969 the marine service was forced to disband, its long history commemorated by the mission's Cessna plane, based in Port McNeill and christened *Columbia V* in memory of the hospital ships.

From the mid 1800s there are records of missionaries of various denominations plying the British Columbia coast by canoe or boat, but there were no hospital ships in those days and the majority of missionaries offered evangelical and not medical service. Catholics, Anglicans, Methodists and Presbyterians were active during this period. 1905 saw the start of the Columbia Coast Mission by John Antle under the auspices of the Anglican Church.

The denominations kept to separate territories for the most part by unofficial agreement. The Methodists (who joined with Congregationalists and 70% of the Presbyterians in 1925 to form the United Church) concentrated on the north, with their most southerly year-round hospital established in Bella Bella in 1898; the Anglicans covered the central area; Roman Catholics were mainly in the southern section. There was no hospital or ambulance service available in the Anglican area from Sechelt to Cape Scott when John Antle began his campaign but, due to his forcefulness and organizing ability, the Columbia Coast Mission during his years as superintendent became by far the largest marine mission on the coast, unique in its year-round, all-weather service, with three hospitals, a travelling hospital ship, and a series of small ambulance ships, all of which patrolled the coastal waters seeking out camps and cabins to give their triple service: medical, social and spiritual.

This is the story of the ships of the Columbia Coast Mission fleet, of the people they served, and of certain of the chaplains, doctors and crew who spent long periods with the fleet or whose tours of duty involved excitement, pathos or comedy. Among the vessels were several with identical names. Following each other in service were *Columbia* I to IV, *John Antle* I to V, and *Rendezvous* I and II. Most of these bore no successive numbers on their hulls and were registered without them, each taking over instead the name of her predecessor, which was sold and renamed by the new owner. The desire of the mission board was always to have a *Columbia, John Antle* and *Rendezvous* on the seas, for tradition's sake and to honour Antle, the founder.

For more than 60 years these hospital and ambulance ships patrolled the coast on routes that took them deep into the long, winding inlets, into little bays, to sparsely settled islands and to storm-battered, rocky isles where lighthouses blinked their warning light to passing vessels. Over ten years have gone by since the last ship was sold and a new era of plane transport superseded the mission boats, but their pioneer service in the days when they answered a crying need should not be forgotten.

2

Love of the sea was in John Antle's blood. He was born in Newfoundland, that bleak, rocky island that has spawned innumerable seamen. He sailed a tiny skiff in the choppy waters of the Atlantic when he was 12 years old, and he sailed a 40-foot yacht from England to Vancouver through submarine-infested seas during World War II when he was 75.

When he was 15, Antle worked one summer on his father's ship, a barquentine sailing out of Harbour Grace in Newfoundland. His father was determined to "put him through the ringbolts", a nautical phrase which meant the boy would receive no favours as the captain's son. He took his turn at long watches and was sent to climb aloft to dizzying heights in the rigging of the ship. It was a rugged introduction to seamanship but the rigorous training stayed with him for a lifetime and explains both the strict discipline he enforced on his ships in later years and the robust language he employed when obstructions delayed his progress. It taught him as well to face the dangers and difficulties he encountered with courage and determination.

Antle's mother was eager for him to enter the ministry, and after obtaining his first class teaching certificate he registered at Queen's Theological College in St. John's, Newfoundland. But Antle was to be no average clergyman headed for a comfortable parishional career. Bold, forceful, quick to flare up with a seaman's strong language, he was destined for a life of adventure, battling storms and battling reluctant business men and organizations for donations to carry on his cherished work.

Something of his courage and self-confidence, perhaps something of the impatience with inefficiency that characterized his career and made him a fascinating but often disconcerting companion, showed up during his student days and in his first years as deacon and priest in the wild west towns of the 1890s.

During Antle's second year at Queen's, a virulent epidemic of smallpox swept through the fishing village of Island Cove, near Harbour Grace. The Spanish brig *William* had arrived in the harbour and the captain, anxious to avoid quarantine, docked without reporting the death of a sailor from smallpox. Certain crew members joined their families in Island Cove and the outbreak soon followed. Mr. Warren, rector and doctor of the little community, was one of the first fatalities.

A message was sent to Queen's College from Bishop Jones of St. John's, requesting a volunteer to take the place of the rector-doctor of Island Cove. Young Antle was the volunteer. He had not been vaccinated until he arrived at the stricken village but escaped the disease despite donning Warren's surplice, which he found hanging in the vestry. He preached for three months until the smallpox epidemic burned itself out. Then, visiting a sick child, he recognized her illness as diphtheria. The child died within four hours and Antle insisted on a graveside service only. Despite protests from the parents and the community that he was burying the child like an animal, he was successful in eliminating an indoor church service that might have started another epidemic. Perhaps this experience was the seed that developed into his conviction that medical and spiritual aid should be a dual service.

His passion for the sea was reawakened when he was sent as deacon to the parish of Greenspond, 200 miles north of Harbour Grace, with transportation entirely by boat along its 75 miles of rugged coastline. In his element here, he carried out his duties with such enthusiasm that an old fisherman said to him, "Well, parson, we've never had a gale on this coast that you haven't been out in."

Antle was not a man to panic, during a storm at sea or in a logging camp, threatened by a burly logger's fist shaken in drunken rage beneath his nose. One dark night he was entering Greenspond harbour in his boat, the *Acolyte*, with two men in a dinghy towing her to her anchorage. Antle was preparing to drop anchor when his foot slipped. He fell overboard, thoroughly entangled in 16 fathoms of chain. He landed on the sea floor, his hands in the mud, his body weighted down and imprisoned by the heavy chain. Swiftly and methodically he worked to disentangle himself and swam to the surface. He found that one of the men, though unable to swim, had leapt from the dinghy to help him and had had to be rescued while Antle was struggling at the bottom of the sea. Antle's injuries kept him in bed for several weeks and he still felt the effects 50 years later.

In 1897 Antle moved west. His parishes in Washington state were an excellent preparation for his rough encounters in the logging camps of British Columbia at the turn of the century. Roslyn was a coal-mining town in Kittitas county, Washington, and known in those days as the toughest of lawless communities. Visiting the home of the postmaster, Antle was shown a fully furnished room with cooking facilities in the basement, to which the family retreated on rowdy occa-

8

sions such as the Fourth of July. Said the postmaster: "To be quite safe from the bullets which are apt to fly a bit too freely around, we have to be below the surface of the ground." To corroborate this, he showed Antle bullet holes in the walls of his house.

In Newfoundland, Antle had never met an unbeliever, but in this mining town he discovered no one who professed a religious faith. His unhappy days in Roslyn explain his realistic attitude towards missionary work in later years. But equally depressing to a sailor was the distance from his love, the sea. He felt stifled in the little town, hemmed in on all sides by snow-peaked mountains. He declared in his Memoirs: "I made a mental vow that as this was the first . . . time that I had been out of sight, sound and smell of the sea, it would also be the last. And so it proved." It was a relief when he was transferred to the parish of Anacortes, which included the surrounding country and the San Juan Islands in the Strait of Juan de Fuca.

Here there was another startling encounter, when he was asked to conduct a burial service on Guemes Island for a man who had been shot to death. He accompanied undertaker and coffin to Guemes, where the coffin was hoisted on a team of horses and taken to the centre of the island. Here, well back in the timber, there was a small cemetery. Antle had prepared a short address for the graveside ceremony, but was taken aback to find a score of villainous looking men surrounding the open grave, each armed with rifle and revolver. Nevertheless, he launched into a speech on the laxity of law enforcement which allowed criminals to go free.

The undertaker and Antle departed on horseback, and as they reached the main road, the undertaker remarked, "Waal, you've got lots of sand. Did you know you were standing on the grave of a murdered man and the murderer was standing directly in front of you with a rifle in the crook of his arm and a revolver in his belt?"

In December 1899, Antle was given the parish of the Fairview district in Vancouver, British Columbia. Services at first were held in the public school at Broadway and Granville

Streets and then in a vacant store until Holy Trinity Church was built on Pine Street between Seventh and Eighth Avenues, a few blocks north of the present church. Now the sea, close at hand, drew him once more. He constructed a 14-foot racing dinghy in his back yard, naming it the *Laverock* (the Scottish word for "lark") after a church ship of Newfoundland on which he had sometimes acted as chaplain. He organized a boys' club resembling today's Sea Scouts, and every Saturday afternoon he relived the days of his youth, putting to sea with his crew of boys, the wind catching his little sail and carrying the *Laverock* swiftly over the waves.

One day in 1903, the Union Steamship vessel *Cassiar* arrived in Vancouver with four dead loggers aboard. The tragic circumstances of their deaths were played up in the newspapers as dramatic copy. Neither doctor nor hospital was available in those northern logging camps, and seriously injured men were forced to travel anywhere from 50 to 350 miles for treatment. In this case, one man had bled to death in an open rowboat, trying to reach the *Cassiar* and get to a Vancouver hospital. Another had died in his bunk, unable to survive the long wait for the little steamer as it made its unhurried way from port to port, maximum speed nine knots, loading and unloading passengers and freight. Many who read the article may have felt a twinge of distress before laying aside their newspapers. To John Antle it was a clarion call to battle, and with his usual alacrity he plunged into action.

First he must "stir up" the church. He instigated the formation of a joint committee of the Dioceses of Columbia, which took in Vancouver Island and adjacent islands, and New Westminster, which included the mainland area of his proposed route for a travelling hospital and missionary ship. The committee authorized him to travel north among the logging camps and remote settlements to confirm the story of the conditions he had described to them. To cover expenses, they bestowed upon him one hundred dollars.

With this largesse, Antle bought a Springfield gas engine, ¾ horsepower, called a "Bull Pup". He installed it in his little *Laverock*, and with his nine-year-old son Vic as crew, set forth on June 2, 1904, to voyage hundreds of miles up the rugged coast, exploring inlets and islands, braving wild weather and treacherous rapids, with only a small scale general chart of Vancouver Island as his guide. He would depend mostly on local information as he travelled the waterways. "There is nothing to worry about the sea if you understand its nature," he said in later years. "It won't hurt you if you obey the rules."[3] But more than one hair-raising experience lay ahead.

3

They left Vancouver in the late afternoon and, propelled by sail and the puny put-put engine, they reached Bowen Island by nightfall and anchored at Cowan's Point. They rolled themselves in blankets and slept in the bottom of the boat, sheltered by a small tent. In the morning they got to Merry Island in Welcome Pass. The lightkeeper, William Franklin, was the first keeper of the station, established in 1903. As Antle talked to him of his hopes for a hospital ship, Franklin mentioned a Dr. Hutton who was pre-empting land at Halfmoon Bay and was trying to make a living by cutting cordwood which was loaded on scows and towed to Vancouver.

Dr. W.A.B. Hutton was a graduate of the University of Manitoba, had been Medical Officer with the Canadian troops in the Riel Rebellion, and later Medical Superintendent of the Garfield Memorial Hospital in Washington, D.C. While there, he was credited with saving the life of the niece of Bishop Philip Brooks of Boston, and after her recovery he married her. Returning to Winnipeg, Hutton became registrar of the university and a successful anaesthetist. Then alcoholism brought his career to a tragic end. His wife committed suicide and Hutton, his life in ruins, came west in a desperate attempt to make a living in the woods. Everyone liked him and spoke well of him, said the lightkeeper, and perhaps he would be the man to work with Antle if the plan materialized.

During his year in Anacortes, Antle had learned of several

men who had lost high positions through alcohol addiction and drifted into the logging camps. The waste of talent had awakened in him then a desire to seek out and aid such men by means of some type of missionary boat. His idea was not to denounce sinners, but to open doors to a return to a fruitful life. He made a note of the name, "Dr. Hutton". This was the man who later became his friend and tireless, versatile helper, the first doctor of the Columbia Coast Mission.

The next day the *Laverock* sailed past Powell River, lingering to see its rushing waterfall. This was six years before the mill and company town were built, and there were no signs of habitation. Here they hooked their first salmon, and after an exciting struggle reeled in the line, only to have it severed on the propeller. The exhausted fish lay on the water, and they paddled quietly towards it, net at the ready. It was almost theirs when a great dogfish swam up swiftly, snatched the salmon and disappeared.

Sliamon, where there was an Indian village and a railroad camp of the Hastings Mill Company, was their first introduction to logging camp meals and the silent dispatch with which loggers speedily consumed their hefty courses. Antle and his boy, despite good appetites, had just finished their soup and were starting on their meat course when the loggers rose as one man, all courses completed, and made for the outdoors to smoke their pipes.

After Lund, the crew of the *Laverock* headed for Johnstone Strait by way of Discovery Passage, undaunted by tales of rapids and tidal bores. They had, after all, a ¾-h.p. Bull Pup engine to carry them through! Gas engines were a novelty in those days and seldom seen in northern waters. As they rounded Cape Mudge on Quadra Island and turned into Discovery Passage, the Scottish lightkeeper, John Davidson, was mystified as he saw the little boat approaching. Later, he said to Antle: "I mind the day when ye kem roond the Cape. Y'r sail was up but it was no pullin' and yet ye gaed along at a guid rate. I was fair surprised till someone tell't me aboot the contraption called the gasoline engine, and then I kenn'd a' aboot ye."[4]

Turning in at Quathiaski Cove on Quadra, Antle met the Pidcock family whose property encompassed most of the cove waterfront. Reginald Pidcock, Indian Agent for the area from Quathiaski to Alert Bay before his death two years previously, had been an ardent Anglican, regularly attending church, or holding services himself where no church was available as he travelled throughout his agency. His widow and grown children welcomed the idea of an Anglican mission ship, and Antle rightly foresaw that this would be one of the families upon whose support he could depend, a friendly oasis in the centre of the area he hoped to serve. "But," he says in his Memoirs, "could I have known the disappointments, the heartbreak, the hell, that I was to endure in making the idea which was slowly forming in my mind a reality, would I not have gone back to my parish in Vancouver and forgotten all but a very thrilling holiday."

Antle had no tide book, indeed these were little known in those days, and he found himself too late for slack water in Seymour Narrows. He and his son climbed to the top of little Maud Island and watched the roaring, surging whirlpools caused by the incoming tide that swept into the narrow passage and broke over massive, submerged Ripple Rock that lay opposite the island. (This was 54 years before the spectacular blasting of the rock.) When the water slowed, the *Laverock* set forth once more, calling at various small logging camps and finally reaching Rock Bay, later the site of the mission's first hospital.

It was Sunday, a calm, sunny day, suggesting church bells and devout parishioners to the young clergyman, but, he relates, "the only sound was a sort of subdued roar coming from the saloon, and occasional groans from perhaps fifty or a hundred loggers lying around on the grass, in all stages of intoxication."[5]

Fired with enthusiasm to raise up so many fallen souls, Antle announced a service to be held in the hotel sitting room, and surprisingly enough a fair number of men staggered in, some having to be supported in their seats by their more sober companions. Little enthusiasm was shown as Antle read a chapter and prayer and tried to lead them in a hymn. But their attention was caught as he began to speak with fervour of his plan to serve them. How many men had bled to death in open boats? he asked them. How many had died while waiting for the weekly freight boat to take them to a doctor and hospital? Plenty.

Passionately he told them: "This is what I want to say to you. I am going to try to alleviate this situation, to give you hospital service so that when you are injured in the woods, you may have a chance for your life. I am going to try to help you intellectually through books and magazines, and spiritually through religious services."[6]

He could say no more, for the men crowded about him, patting him on the back and seizing his arms and carrying him along with them to the saloon. For the first time in his life the clergyman stood at a bar while the jubilant loggers demanded, "What's yer poison? Name your tipple!"

Despite Antle's confident air of superiority, ever conscious of his own intelligence and education, there was enough of the rugged seaman about him to put him at ease with working men. He declined a drink but admitted to a desire for a smoke and they stuffed his pockets with cigars. He smoked them manfully, though longing for his pipe, and listened as the loggers related with relish the story of a Toronto divine who had visited Rock Bay. During his sermon, the clergyman had paused to remonstrate with a drunken logger who had collapsed to the floor and uttered a loud profanity as he lay prostrate. The logger listened patiently as the learned theologian stood over him, lecturing him sternly and at length on the evils of bad language and liquor. When he concluded his reproof there was a moment of silence, broken by the logger who suddenly burst into such a stream of colourful swear words that the congregation broke into applause and the service ended in confusion. Not for nothing had a Vancouver lawyer described Rock Bay on a Sunday as "It put Hell to blush."[7]

Antle, however, smoked his second cigar and listened to a logger describe the flora of British Columbia to him, pointing out plants that grew wild about the camp and giving their botanical names. "A man in his overalls is not to be hastily adjudged an ignoramus," Antle wrote. "He may know more about many things than oneself." He resolved, "There's no use preaching...I'm going to build a ship and show these fellows there is something worth living for besides whisky."

Alert Bay in 1904 consisted of the Indian village, the cannery, the mission and Indian industrial school and half a dozen houses. All were strung along the waterfront with its spectacular view of small fir-clad islands backed by the snow-peaked ranges of northern Vancouver Island to the west. Alfred Hall of the Church Missionary Society was acting as minister and school superintendent when Antle arrived there. A.W. Corker, the teacher, was absent on leave. Antle felt the spiritual and educational needs of the Indian boys were well served, but was horrified by the neglect of their health.

Missionaries were supposed to know the rudiments of medicine, but Antle knew well that "a little learning is a dangerous thing." Everywhere he saw emaciated, tubercular Indians, some crippled or paralytic. At dinner in the industrial school, he saw a boy at the next table whose head and neck were covered with suppurating sores. No attempt was made to isolate him, and Mr. Hall replied to Antle's enquiries with: "What can I do? There is no doctor in the place." Antle quoted this when he strove some years later to prove to the Minister of the Interior in Ottawa the need for a doctor and hospital in Alert Bay.

No towns as such existed north of Comox in those days. There were long stretches of uninhabited wilderness for the *Laverock* to cover before human contact was made. Word of a small logging camp up one of the deep inlets would send them searching, but as the camps were frequently built on rafts to be moved easily from one location to another, the camp would be gone and the search would continue.

On the return trip, the weather changed and rain poured down in torrents on the open boat, seeping under the tent and soaking the captain and his small crew member. At Port Neville they anchored near the Hansen ranch. Years later,

Mrs. Hansen recalled the arrival of the *Laverock*. Little Victor, cold and wet, clad in knee pants and socks, came up to the house with a large teapot and asked if she would fill it with hot water. Instead, she sent her husband Hans to the beach to bring Antle and his wet blankets to the house to dry out by the big old round cookstove and enjoy a hot meal.

Hans Hansen, born in Norway, was well known on the coast as "Hans the Boatman" for the skilful way he ran his small boat, using a sail and one oar. He had lost a hand in an accident and had it replaced with a hook shaped to fit his oar. Hansen moved to Port Neville in 1891 and became its first postmaster four years later. The Hansens were pioneering when Antle first visited them and the home was a little shack. In future years when there was a large house and prosperous farm the warm welcome continued for any chaplain of the Columbia Coast Mission who anchored in that scenic harbour.

Antle and his son rested and dried out for several days in the hospitable spot, then sailed on through Sunderland Channel, Whirlpool Rapids and Greene Point Rapids to Shoal Bay, a busy centre, though no longer the boom town it had been in early mining days. At their stop at a logging camp in Frederick Arm, Antle received an enthusiastic response to his news of the proposed medical service, and in return he was told gruesome tales of accidents in the woods and of deaths due to lack of medical aid. Lonely graves all along the coast of these isolated areas bore witness to the truth of the stories.

Now the dread Yaculta Rapids by Stuart Island lay ahead, rapids whose whirlpools had spun the Spanish schooner *Sutil* three times round in a circle back in 1792, until the explorer Galiano wrote in his diary, "those on board were made giddy." Many a life had been lost when impatient travellers tried to go through the wild waters without waiting for slack tide. Antle rose early to make a start in time to reach the Yacultas, several miles south, at the time of slack tide, but as he was about to start his engine the camp foreman came down and urged him not to disappoint the loggers who were expecting father and son to join them for breakfast. Antle had intended to skip breakfast, not trusting the stability of his stove, a converted coal-oil tin, if the going was rough, but he was persuaded to return to the camp and share the loggers' hearty meal.

To his dismay, when they reached the rapids a flood tide was running strongly. The two-mile course was crooked and Antle was unable to see what dangers might lie ahead. He decided to chance it. In a moment they were into the swift tide, and soon could see whirls and turmoil in the waters beyond Dent Island. Antle knew he had been wrong in entering these unknown rapids at their most dangerous period, but now it was too late; they were in for it. He called to his boy to inflate his air cushion and hang on to it if anything happened, and this warning roused the child's terror as the boat spun out of control in the whirlpools. Antle tells of their frightening experience:

"We skimmed along the edge of several big ones, looking with dread into their funnel-like depths, with the question in our minds: How long before we shall take a header into one? Sure enough, almost immediately we found our little vessel at an angle of 30 or 40 degrees, skimming around the edge of a big one. Finally we crashed to the bottom of it with a bang against a chunk of wood, which shook every timber in the little ship. The boy was yelling at the top of his voice and grabbed his cushion, while I, less articulate but just as scared, wondered how far down we should go. But to our great surprise and relief the smash into the bottom of the pool destroyed its whirling motion and we were suddenly on a flat surface, the engine and sail both still doing business. Verily, there is a Providence who takes care of children and fools, and both were in that boat."

They rested for a day and night at Camp Island, near Cortes, visiting Charlie Strange and his two sisters, former parishioners of Antle's church. Shortly after this the Stranges moved to Cortes.

A westerly wind that sped the *Laverock* on her way became a howling gale as the sailboat fled before it to Vancouver. Little Vic was miserably seasick, and Antle himself felt far from chipper as they sailed into port on June 29. "But we did it," he says, "and that was that." He settled down to write his report for the joint committee of the Dioceses of New Westminster and Columbia.

4

Antle's report to the joint committee told of visiting 12 settlements and 12 logging camps, and emphasized the enthusiastic reception he had received at Rock Bay logging camp and the expressed desire for Anglican services on Quadra Island. In his usual blunt manner, wasting no time through diplomacy where he felt himself right, he told them missionary work among the loggers had failed so far because only religious services had been offered, "which", he said, "in my opinion is putting the thick end of the wedge first."

To bring the church into contact with the loggers, the work must be largely social at first, and for this he suggested three ideas for which the men had expressed their approval: a circulating library, a hospital, and a monthly magazine with news of the various camps, by means of which the missionary in charge could reach every man on the coast. But the work must be done soon, he urged. The men expected it, the idea had been publicized, delay would mean disappointment and perhaps some other church not as well equipped for the work would step in ahead and take over.

To Antle, with his energy and enthusiasm, it seemed that all should be fair sailing. He had prepared plans for a 60-foot boat with 14-foot beam and 4½-foot depth, with good sleeping quarters for a crew of three and a main cabin large enough to accommodate congregations of 25 or 30 persons. He had included a little cupboard which opened to reveal an altar complete with dossal (the silk cloth hanging behind the altar), altar cloth and cross. The Diocese of New Westminster expressed approval, but in Victoria, before the committee of the Diocese of Columbia, he encountered objections that infuriated him.

The committee felt the initial cost and upkeep would be prohibitive. One man suggested a rowboat that could be pulled up on the beach would be a better idea. Another offered a 30-foot boat of his own that he wanted to sell. A third suggested use of a sealing schooner at present tied up in Vancouver harbour and advertised for sale.

Impatiently, Antle disposed of these impractical suggestions. A rowboat, he said scornfully, was scarcely an adequate operating room for a doctor, and he doubted if any doctor would consider spending a rainy night on the beach under shelter of an overturned boat. Similarly, the 30-foot motorboat had no cabin for a doctor's consultations, and the sealing schooner would need at least six men to handle her and a good gasoline engine to keep her from being swept ashore in storms and strong currents.

Disgusted with the absurd suggestions that threatened to delay or defeat his cherished project, a project for which he was prepared to give up his comfortable post at Holy Trinity to implement, Antle exclaimed fiercely: "Gentlemen, these are my plans. I am not a cheap man and I will not touch a cheap outfit. Good evening." And he left the room abruptly.

His forceful presentation and angry departure eventually swayed the committee, and he was told the following day that his ideas had been accepted in entirety. He was commissioned to go east to Toronto and apply to the Missionary Society of the Church in Canada for a grant to build the boat. It was the first of many such appeals that Antle was forced to make over the years to build and maintain his ships, and in this case he was successful.

He returned in triumph, work commenced at once in Wallace Shipyards in Vancouver, and Antle was appointed superintendent of the newly formed Columbia Coast Mission. In 1907 the mission was incorporated under the Friendly Societies Act with a Board of Directors and an Executive Committee. The Bishop of British Columbia was chairman of the board[8] and Antle was responsible to him. The board made the final decisions on staff appointments and the allotting of finances.

The launching of the *Columbia* from Wallace Shipyards in False Creek was a gala event. Wallace Shipyards was run by the father of Clarence Wallace, later Lieutenant-Governor of British Columbia, who as a small boy was present at the ceremony. A huge crowd of over 1000 spectators jammed the wharf on April 4, 1905, as Archdeacon Pentreath conducted the service, assisted by city clergy and a boys' choir. On board at the launching were John Antle and Dr. Hutton, whom Antle had contacted and persuaded to join the enterprise as ship's doctor and engineer. Antle had brought Hutton to his Fairview home where he lived with the Antles for several months during construction of the *Columbia*.

Objections had been made by some to the use of champagne to christen a missionary ship, and eventually it was decided to use a bottle of Lithia water, tinfoiled about the neck to resemble champagne. Antle's wife christened the ship, and the face of a workman who caught a section of the bottle as it broke and sampled the contents was a study in chagrin. The *Columbia*, with Antle's two little boys also aboard, slid into the water neatly and without mishap, but the next day was found to be half full of water. Dr. Hutton commented wryly to Antle: "What can you expect but defective waterworks when you give a boat Lithia water at her launching?"

Antle made his trial run with her on April 15 to the accompaniment of dire predictions of shipwreck if the engine failed and left the *Columbia* at the mercy of winds, tides and currents. It was felt that a 60-foot vessel should never be dependent on one of the new, unpredictable gasoline engines. However, the 20-h.p. Union engine gave no trouble, the trip was a success and the crew returned triumphant. On three occasions during her term of service, the gasoline-powered *Columbia* towed to port three disabled steamboats, and Antle chronicled each event with satisfaction in the mission magazine, *The Log*.

On April 28 the ship was dedicated in Victoria by Bishop Perrin, assisted once more by clergy and choir, with Lieutenant-Governor Sir Henri Joly de Lotbinière and some 350 guests present at the ceremony. While the *Columbia* was in

Victoria, it was decided to run an excursion to try out the ship once again. One of the guests was the well-known Captain Walbran, author in 1909 of *British Columbia Coast Names* and master of the steam-powered D.G.S. *Quadra*. This was Walbran's first experience with a boat powered by an internal combustion engine, often called in those days an "infernal" combustion engine due to its unreliability.

On the return trip Captain Walbran came into the wheel-house to watch the landing, viewing with great misgiving the combination of a missionary captain and the unpredictable gas engine. As the *Columbia* neared the dock, Antle rang the stop bell and Dr. Hutton as engineer threw out the clutch to stop the propeller. Walbran was accustomed to silence from his steam engine when he rang his bell on the *Quadra*. As the *Columbia*'s engine ran merrily on and the dock grew ever nearer, Walbran could not contain himself and breaking all rules of naval etiquette he shouted to Antle: "Stop your engines, man! You'll ram the dock!"

"All in good time, captain," Antle answered calmly, rang two bells to go astern, and berthed his ship neatly. Walbran apologized profusely and afterwards whenever they met he referred to his panic on his introduction to the gas engine.

Gas engines were baulky pieces of machinery in those early days. The *Columbia* caused her crew plenty of trouble during her first runs up the coast, but Hutton, though no mechanic, grew to know her engine's idiosyncracies and was always able to coax it to life. His enthusiasm for the *Columbia* and her work rivalled that of Antle. He declared he would never leave the ship, and often said, "When I die I want to be buried at sea from the *Columbia*."

They were eager to get started, and as the boat received her final fittings, Antle exclaimed, "The minute we are ready, we'll go—night or day." The *Columbia* was ready for them at 5 p.m. on May 9, and they set off immediately, excited and resolute despite some qualms of what might lie ahead in those wilderness logging camps whose men sometimes liked to refer to themselves as "timber beasts". But the scenery on the whole of the route was breathtaking as they wended their way through a myriad of forested islands, with the great mountains of the Coast Range on their starboard side and the sea breeze salty and invigorating.

Antle waxed lyrical on occasion, describing the sensational scenery. "Switzerland and Norway rolled into one could not rival Bute Inlet for wild and rugged scenery," he wrote in *The Log*. "Imagine an immense fiord, from one to two miles wide, stretching its sinuous length forty miles into the heart of the Coast Range. On every side, as one proceeds, are mountains, rising almost sheer from the water, to a height sometimes of 8000 feet, with sides patched with timber, and summits capped with clouds of everlasting snow. On either side of the course are seen foaming cascades descending with a roar into the sea..."[9]

One of their first calls had been at Merry Island on May 10, 1905, where Antle and Hutton signed the visitors' book of lightkeeper William Franklin who had been instrumental in bringing the two of them together. The entry reads: "Rev. Antle. Dr. W.A.B. Hutton. Mission Ship Columbia."

Quarters on the first *Columbia* were less than commodious. There were two small staterooms, each just large enough to hold a bunk, for Antle and Hutton. In the main cabin, two hospital cots stood behind curtains, and the operating table and dispensary rubbed elbows with the library and the altar. In these crowded quarters the captain, doctor and deckhand ate their meals, with Dr. Hutton keeping an eye on his patients and an ear alert for faltering sounds from the gas engine. One deckhand left the ship for good when they docked in Vancouver, unable to take the combination of southeaster storms and, on this particular trip, a cabin shared with two typhoid patients, brought to Vancouver because the hospital that Antle had speedily built was overcrowded. An occasional retreat to privacy, which Antle found essential to his well-being, was virtually impossible. From the first tour of the 54 camps on his agenda, Antle knew a larger ship would soon be needed.

But the little *Columbia* was kept busy from the start, treating her first case on board on May 14. During the following eight months the doctor gave out 334 prescriptions, performed 18 operations on board and ran numerous severe cases to the well-equipped Queen's Hospital at Rock Bay, the first of the Columbia Coast Mission hospitals.

5

A hospital in the centre of the northern logging camps was an integral part of Antle's plan, with the ship treating emergency and minor cases on board and conveying severe cases swiftly to a hospital that was within easy reach, thus eliminating what might be a week's wait for the freight boat and a long trip down to a Vancouver hospital. As soon as the *Columbia*'s route was established, Antle began another of his never-ending quests for financial aid.

He went to Charles M. Beecher, a head of the Hastings Mill Company, and presented his scheme for a hospital at the site of their large logging camp at Rock Bay. Beecher showed little interest. These were the early days of logging; conditions were rough, safety rules were unknown and camp operators felt no obligation to guard the welfare of their employees.

Antle, ending an impassioned plea, exclaimed: "Mr. Beecher, a hospital is going to be built on the coast and the question for you to decide is whether or not your company, the largest operating on the coast, can afford to stand out of the movement."

There was a pause, and then Beecher said, "I like your spirit. Sit down and we'll talk some more." He promised to give Antle his decision later on. The day arrived for the meeting of the committee formed to discuss hospital possibilities. No word had come from Beecher, and despondency reigned. Then a telephone call came for Antle. It was Beecher, announcing that the Hastings Mill Company would build the hospital and contribute $100 to the boat fund.

The work progressed speedily, and Queen's Hospital opened on July 9, 1905, joining the store, liquor saloon and hotel at this headquarters of Hastings Mill. The Victorian Order of

Nurses supplied the nursing staff of two: Miss Jean Sutherland as Head Nurse and Miss Alice Franklin as her assistant. The order also furnished the rooms, while the mission paid the salaries of the nursing staff and supplied the surgeon, drugs, instruments and food. The nurses arrived on S.S. *Cassiar* the day before the ceremony, along with Archdeacon Pentreath who officially opened the building. There were patients in the ten-bed hospital before the opening ceremony, and in the first eight months the hospital performed 33 operations, treated 45 surgical cases, dispensed 228 prescriptions and delivered three babies. Dr. Hutton served as surgeon for both the *Columbia* and the hospital and trained John Antle to be his anaesthetist.

One of the first accidents treated on the *Columbia* is typical of the peculiar cases they were apt to encounter, and proved to be an eye-opener for a young English clergyman who was a guest on board. The ship was anchored at Bear River when a boat came alongside with a man who had been struck by the falling limb of a tree. To stem the flow of blood, the loggers in the camp had plastered his head with flour, and this had hardened, forming a bloody helmet which the doctor had to remove before locating the severed artery and pinching and tying it. By the time this was done, Hutton and Antle were covered in blood and the young clergyman, overcome by the gruesome sight, was in the process of losing his dinner over the rail.

A sense of humour, and the ability to appreciate comedy even at the expense of oneself was essential to survive the pressures experienced on the mission boat. Antle never forfeited his dignity but he enjoyed a good story. One that he often told was of a Sunday evening when he had gathered a number of the Rock Bay loggers together on the *Columbia* for a service. He was about to start his sermon when a knock came at the door. A logger from the Bear River camp had made a laborious trip through the woods and then come eight miles by boat to report a man run over by a logging train. Antle apologized to his congregation, saying he must skip the sermon and leave at once for Bear River. As the *Columbia* pulled out, the boom man shouted to Antle, "By God, that's the best sermon I ever heard in my life!"

The injured logger, Eric Nye, had jumped from the rear of the logging train and the caulks on his boots had wedged themselves into the wooden sleeper, holding him fast. The train backed up, knocking him down and passing over him, its wooden brake beams hitting him over and over. An arm and leg were broken, and the wounds in his scalp needed 37 stitches. Miraculously, he recovered in the Rock Bay hospital. During one period, the *Columbia* took a wounded logger to hospital from various camps every night for eight nights in a row. Antle called the Bear River camp by Port Neville one of the finest camps on the coast, for "Indian women are not allowed to prowl around and no liquor is allowed in the camp."[10]

Dr. Hutton acted, or attempted to act, as a restraining force at times on Antle's impetuosity. The liquor problem in particular exasperated Antle. He was deeply fond of Dr. Hutton, who enjoyed his glass, but Hutton never overindulged during his blissful year on the *Columbia.* Antle could stand at the bar beside the Rock Bay loggers while they toasted his health, without breaking into a tirade against drink. But an indulgence that led to ill health, immorality and inability to work to one's fullest capacity roused his ire and a determination to set things right.

One morning the *Columbia* turned into the landlocked harbour of Granite Bay on Quadra Island where Hastings Mill ran one of its camps. Antle went over to talk to the men who were roping the logs into booms, ready for towing. As he chatted, Antle glanced across the bay to where there was an Indian encampment with scarlet blankets strung on a line, waving in the breeze against a background of evergreens. He commented on the beauty of the picture, and the foreman replied dryly, "You wouldn't think it such a pretty picture if you had to listen to the screeching that wakes us every morning around four o'clock."

It seems the young Indian girls visited the logging camp at night, taking with them whisky to sell and returning home in

THE COLUMBIA IS COMING!

the early morning. As they were always reluctant to part with the money they made from liquor and prostitution, their irate husbands would beat the shrieking girls unmercifully until they turned over every penny. This was a correct procedure, the men felt, for they needed the money for their potlatches.

Antle determined to put a stop to what he called "the nefarious custom carried on by some of the Indians of selling their women for immoral purposes to the white men."[11] Hutton strongly advised him not to interfere, saying he had no authority here and "your hands are full enough already." "If I have no authority, I'll use bluff," Antle replied. He walked over to the Indian encampment and demanded that they leave the district at once. The Indians explained they were berry-picking on their ancestral grounds, but Antle said sternly they must be gone by seven the next morning or he would inform the Indian Agent. Evidently impressed by the *Columbia*, which they may have believed to be a government boat, the Indians loaded their canoes sharp at seven o'clock and paddled away, to Hutton's astonishment and Antle's relief and satisfaction.

The troubles that Hutton had predicted followed fast, and Antle leapt boldly into the thick of the fray. He related the incident in *The Log* magazine and, up and down the coast, Indians, squaw men and loggers argued Antle's action pro and con. The Hastings Mill loggers, at first resentful, were persuaded by those who were in sympathy with him that as a missionary he could not have done otherwise. Buoyed by their support, Antle went to the district Indian Agent and asked for his help. In agreement at first, the agent later wrote to say he did not feel called upon to spend his time "chasing Indian whores around the coast." Angrily, Antle sought out Bishop Perrin in Victoria, who concurred with Hutton that the fiery chaplain would ruin the mission if he interfered in such matters. "The mission is ruined already if I don't," replied Antle, and persuaded the bishop to go with him to the office of the inspector of Indian Agencies.

Here fire met fire as the inspector delivered a tirade ending, "I'm sick and tired of young parsons with a vision coming here to tell a man of my age what to do about the Indians!"

"I'm sick too of seeing men in your position, drawing a big salary and doing nothing to earn it. You do nothing for the Indians..." Antle retorted.

The gentle bishop, greatly distressed, tried to restrain Antle, but the inspector, calming down, surprised them by saying to the missionary, "You are the right man for the job; from now on I'll assist you," and promising to donate several cases of books to the *Columbia*'s library.

In his account in *The Log* of the Indian campsite incident, Antle had criticized squaw men who lived common law with Indian women, saying if a woman was good enough to live with a man and bear his children, she was good enough for him to marry. A young French Canadian, Napoleon LeClair, read this statement, unconventional for the times. He was devoted to his little daughter and her Indian mother and sent word to Antle that despite his parents' objection he wanted to be married. As the *Columbia* approached his home, LeClair and the Indian woman rowed out to meet the ship in a howling snowstorm, and the ceremony took place in the *Columbia*'s chapel. The groom had neglected to bring a ring, and Dr. Hutton, acting as the best man, produced one that had been his mother's wedding ring.

Antle's complex personality offended some and baffled many more. He was proud, courageous, forceful and passionate, as intolerant of opposition as of ineptitude, and yet compassionate towards suffering and sympathetic to genuine need. Reserved and devout, he used a seaman's robust language when his wrath was kindled.

His assumption that only his own ideas were correct and their implementation essential is shown in his first annual report on January 3, 1906, to the board to which he was responsible, and whose members included prelates of the two dioceses and clergy and prominent citizens of the areas. The board's chief interest was in spiritual matters, and it held the purse strings and decided on policy. But that very self-assurance of Antle's gave him the driving force to push through his plans despite men who quibbled and procrastinated. There is nothing tentative or servile in these extracts:

"Church Work.—It must be understood that in so large a district, and with a population so varied in creed and nationality, it is very difficult to introduce church work in the way of regular church services, and not always judicious even when possible. I have found by experience that it is never well to push church services upon people who are not prepared for them. When they are in a condition to be benefitted then they will ask for them...

"Literature.—...Though the men in the camps as a class are readers, and many of them intelligent readers, no regular provision had ever been made to supply them with literature until this mission was started....We get a large number of magazines and some books, but not regularly, and a large quantity are entirely out of date and useless. We often get stacks of 'Delineators', 'Weldon's Ladies' Journal', and other fashion papers, of very ancient date at that, which not being considered of any use as mental food to an able-bodied logger, are usually committed to the deep. I think that as the churches are apparently too busy with their own affairs to do this work, it is the duty of this committee to deal with the matter...

"Medical—...This committee will still have to push forward, to enlarge its borders, to occupy new ground, or better it had never begun the work...work of which the church might do more, if she would learn to obey the first missionary order: 'Heal the sick.'..."

Antle had not forgotten his plan to bring social as well as medical and spiritual comfort to the isolated areas. The first of many concerts and picnics put on by the mission boats was at Rock Bay on February 17, 1906. Loggers from Camps A, B, and D across the lake were asked to join the Rock Bay contingent, and a special engine was detailed to bring in from the woods those who wished to attend. In the mess room, decorated with flags from the *Columbia,* they found waiting an orchestra consisting of two loggers (John Shortreed and Ed Bowron) with violins, one (Charlie Newberg) with a guitar, and Antle with his little portable organ. Quartets, trios and solos were played, and recitations, readings and songs followed, each greeted with applause by men bored with the monotony of logging camp life.

"I hope this is only the beginning of things in this line," said Antle, and over the years these concerts, always including a brief service by the chaplain, were expanded until they became highlights in the lives of men, women and children in lonely areas of the coast, brought together by the mission boat to enjoy the society of fellow settlers.

The literature distributed increased in volume and quality. Books by standard authors were supplied to the camps in boxes fitted with shelves, the boxes containing 20 to 50 books according to the size of the camp. These were consigned to the custody of the foreman and regularly exchanged for a new selection. Mr. C. Jenner Hogg helped Antle with the library selection and distribution.

Though the Columbia Coast Mission was supposedly non-sectarian in its organization, the *Columbia* was essentially an Anglican missionary ship and the chief interest of the church in Vancouver and Victoria was to see an increase in Anglicans. Antle held services whenever he could collect even the smallest of groups. There were numerous baptisms and marriage ceremonies, and pictures of the participants were printed in *The Log* and distributed up and down the coast. One marriage in September of 1906 was performed by Antle between Mary Emily Pidcock, daughter of former Indian Agent R.H. Pidcock, and John Cecil Smith, known as Cougar Smith because of the 800 cougars he had shot. (A road off the Island Highway is named after him.) A year later their infant, Gwendolyn Mary Cecil, was baptized on board the *Columbia*. In the 1930s, Gwendolyn became a nurse for the Columbia Coast Mission.

During the months of the *Columbia*'s construction, Antle had confided to his house guest, Dr. Hutton, his misgivings about the success of missionary work among the loggers. During his *Laverock* tour, some had shown enthusiasm for the idea of a hospital ship, but there was little or no interest displayed in plans for religious services. Was he, as a missionary, justified in raising money for what might only be medical aid? Hutton reassured him in his bluff, good-natured manner by quoting St Luke: "'Heal the sick . . . and say unto them, the kingdom of God is come nigh unto you.' Take that for your text," he said. "Heal their bodies and the rest will follow."

The text became a slogan for the Columbia Coast Mission ships, and Antle quoted it in his first report to the board. One of his first tasks was to collect a number of empty cookie tins, fill them with first-aid supplies and donate them, along with instructions, to the various logging camps. Such supplies had never been kept in the camps, and someone's old shirt, not always clean, was usually torn up for an accident victim, or as in that early case, the wound was packed with flour!

In July 1906, Dr. William Allan was appointed to take over the Queen's Hospital work, allowing Hutton to devote himself to the ship. That month, Hutton arranged to take a long-overdue holiday, accepting an offer to travel as chemist with a group going to Blunden Harbour to investigate the possibilities of setting up commercial oyster beds. Aboard the tug *Chehalis*, the group set sail from North Vancouver. There was a strong tide flooding into the harbour and, as the tug was opposite Brockton Point, the Canadian Pacific steamer *Princess Victoria*, entering the harbour, swerved out of her course in the strong current and rammed the tug, sinking her. Eight of those aboard, including Dr. Hutton, went down with the *Chehalis*, and neither tug nor bodies were ever recovered.

Thus Antle lost a good friend and faithful worker, whose avowed ambition had been to spend the rest of his life on the *Columbia* and be buried at sea from her decks. Antle attempted to start a fund among Winnipeg doctors for a mission ship to be called the *W.A. Hutton* after the doctor who had done so much for the enterprise in its earliest and most difficult stage. He was unsuccessful, but later a monument was erected in Stanley Park near the Brockton Point light-house in memory of the *Chehalis* victims.

Dr. D.P. Hanington, a graduate of McGill, came from the

Royal Victoria Hospital in Montréal to take Dr. Hutton's place on the *Columbia*. Antle picked him up in Victoria and they set out at once for the north. Hanington had brought along his little dog, Honey, which was experiencing its first sea voyage and ran about the ship in bewilderment, causing its master great anxiety. The *Columbia* had just passed Prospect Point lighthouse on her way out of the harbour when the doctor rushed into the wheelhouse shouting, "Honey is overboard!"

Antle pulled the wheel hard over, turned about, and sailed slowly back to Brockton Point, scanning the waters intently with binoculars. No Honey could be seen. Giving the dog up for lost, Antle headed the ship once more for the north, thinking up consoling words that he would offer his new doctor when they met at supper. Suddenly Hanington appeared once more in the wheelhouse, exclaiming happily, "Captain, Honey is all right. She was shut up in my cabin." No words of congratulation came from the captain, who stared grimly ahead. Time, gasoline and sympathy wasted, he reported glumly in *The Log*.

Antle may have acquired a more charitable view of the doctor a few weeks later when a violent northwest wind struck them at four in the morning where they lay anchored by Camp K at Thurlow Island. The *Columbia* was pounding so hard against the float that Antle decided the only recourse was to put to sea before she was smashed to pieces. The violent wind was blowing directly into the cove, with the ship broadside to it, and getting her head to the wind would be a difficult task.

Hanington started up the engine and, since their deckhand had left them before this trip, Antle stationed Joe, the Chinese cook, by the line with his meat cleaver at the ready. When a momentary lull came, Antle rang for full speed ahead, Joe chopped the line, and the *Columbia* struggled head on into the wind and around the point, where they went "careering down the channel with the wind howling behind" to Shoal Bay. Throughout the mad ride, Hanington ran back and forth from engine room to cabin, trying to bring order into the chaos that had resulted when the buffeting burst open the

THE COLUMBIA IS COMING!

sliding doors of the library and spilled books all over the floor, as well as overturning furniture. It was a rough initiation for a city man but Hanington seems to have worked hard on ship and in hospital, and letters to *The Log* from camp supervisors express gratitude for the doctor's care of accident victims.

One such case concerned a serious accident up Sunderland Channel at Norton and McKinnon's camp, when one man was killed and another badly injured. Fortunately, Antle was visiting the camp with the *Columbia* and was spending the evening talking to one of the supervisors, George Fraser. William Norton and the new foreman, Jack Bennett, had gone up the hill after supper to blast out a stump with dynamite. The blast rang out, seeming unusually loud. When nearly an hour had elapsed without the reappearance of the men, Fraser sent Pat Rogers and several others up the chute with lanterns to investigate. Antle went back on board the *Columbia* to wait for prearranged signals.

Up in the woods the steam whistle of the donkey engine sounded, and Antle responded with the *Columbia*'s powerful whistle. Within five minutes Antle, Dr. Hanington and an assistant were climbing the chute along with a dozen more men.

Norton was found nearly 40 feet from the stump, badly mangled and nearly frozen to death, but still conscious. Coats, blankets and hot water bottles were piled on him and the doctor applied emergency treatment for a broken jaw, injured arm and severe cuts. The body of Bennett, torn apart by the blast, was discovered nearly an hour later, 80 feet away in the brush.

A grateful letter from George Fraser to *The Log* ended: "On behalf of the thirty odd men in camp, I am requested to express their most heartfelt gratitude to the captain of the *Columbia* for holding her here until Saturday when the patient was able to be moved to the hospital. Also I am instructed to put down in good plain English the most emphatic approval of Dr. Hanington's splendid work in the two days and nights he was at the bedside, and am to 'see that they print it in the *Log*'. Therefore I make the request that our thanks be expressed in our own way and if I may be permitted a line on my own account, it is to say that nothing but the most intelligent care and professional skill could have saved our employer's life."

In other areas Dr. Hanington put forth similar effort. At a Christmas party on the *Columbia* for children of Quathiaski Cove where Mrs. Blackall of the cannery store played the ship's organ and the young Yeatman boys gave recitations, it is recorded that Hanington "sang college songs until hoarse."

The concert was in aid of the new hospital at Van Anda, a small mining town near the north end of Texada Island. The Tacoma Steel Company which ran the Marble Bay mine at Van Anda had asked Antle to establish a hospital there, and supplied an old dance hall at a low rent. This the mission converted into a ten-bed hospital named Columbia and officially opened in 1907 by Bishop W.W. Perrin. Dr. Keith and Dr. J.H. MacDermott of Vancouver were the first doctors appointed, and nurses were Miss Beatty and Miss E. Franklin (sister to Alice Franklin, nurse at Queen's Hospital, Rock Bay.) That same year, Queen's Hospital was doubled in size. It now contained 20 beds, and the new wing was furnished once again by the Victorian Order of Nurses. Dr. Hanington was appointed surgeon.

Whaletown on Cortes Island, the old whaling station of the 1860s, was one of the *Columbia*'s ports of call in the early 1900s, and its settlers were for the most part receptive to the mission boat. Antle was usually sure of a little congregation in the ship's chapel when he anchored there. On one occasion an elderly pioneer, Mr. Robertson, felt disinclined to hear the sermon but tossed a silver dollar through the skylight to express his support. It fell at Antle's feet. "Manna from heaven!" exclaimed the startled chaplain.

The David Robertsons had settled in Whaletown on Cortes in 1905. Their daughter, Mrs. M.A. Shaw, writes: "It was quite isolated then...We looked forward to the visits of the *Columbia* and the services on board. First the *Columbia* under Rev. Antle, and later Rev. Alan Greene, who became a close friend of my family... The services were frequently held in our home, and neighbours' homes too. Our community Christmas tree parties with gifts and refreshments were sponsored by the C.C. Mission, and a big event in our early days."[12]

Throughout 1907 the *Columbia*'s crew kept to her crowded schedule, visiting settlements and conducting services, baptizing babies and performing wedding ceremonies, while the doctor treated the patients who came to the boat. Lists of the injured were published in *The Log* for some years. A few of those listed in October 1906 included Jack Whipple, Camp D, struck by chain hook, lost most of foot; William Lewis of Paterson's camp, injured thumb, 14 stitches; C. Berlingson, Beaver Creek, fell with a tree, internal injuries and broken wrist; I. Teepan of Cracroft Island, broken collarbone; and Pat Diffley, broken rib, torn lung. Sturdy John Norberg of Thurlow Island Logging Camp refused chloroform when operated on for a severe axe wound. "Like most loggers he regards the chloroform bottle with a mixture of suspicion and contempt," said *The Log* of October 1906.

Among the guests on the *Columbia* in October of 1907 was the Reverend A.H. Sovereign of Christ Church, Vancouver, (later Bishop of Yukon) who experienced his first visit to a logging camp. Fifty-four camps were visited that month by the *Columbia*. Doctors serving on the ship during those first years included Doctors W. Allan, Alan Beech and J.W. Auld.

The *Columbia* arranged her schedule to meet S.S. *Cassiar* when she called at Shoal Bay on her up trip, collected mail for the mission ship's crew and also for Rock Bay, then ran the loggers' mail back to the camp in time for the men to answer their letters and give the replies to the *Cassiar* on her way down. Camps sent a list of unclaimed letters to *The Log* which published the names for loggers who had moved on to other camps.

Antle put forth a scheme in an editorial in *The Log* whereby loggers could pay $1-a-month hospital fee for year-round service. The money would enable the *Columbia* to call more frequently at the camps, perhaps every ten days. Such frequent collections proved difficult, and yearly tickets of $10 were substituted. The insurance plan worked well at first, but ran into trouble when competition arose with the United Brotherhood of America.

The good relationship between Antle and the Rock Bay loggers was strained for a few years following the opening of their hospital, when Antle plunged into a crusade against the coast saloons. Loggers at this time were unable to cash cheques in their company stores, but could in the liquor saloons, which often encouraged them to drink up most of their pay cheques. Sermons by Antle had no effect. Logging camp operator Allison at Chatham Channel expressed his forebodings to Antle when a saloon was planned for Minstrel Island. The saloon at nearby Port Harvey was already drawing many of his workers. Antle saw a loophole in the fact that a number of saloons were operating falsely under hotel licences, and persuaded Attorney-General Bowser to refuse their licence renewals. This caused a great uproar and opened the way for the arrival on the scene of the United Brotherhood of America.

Vigorously opposing Antle and the mission, the U.B.A. offered a health insurance scheme whereby loggers could receive treatment at any hospital for an initial payment of $5 and a yearly fee of $12. Hundreds joined, Rock Bay loggers alone paying out $12,000 in one summer. However, little or none of the insurance money was paid to the mission hospitals which treated the men. After three years, the U.B.A. manager disappeared, leaving about $3000 owing to doctors, hospitals, undertakers and grocers. There were no assets. The bitterness engendered by the struggle took some years to fade, but Antle felt he had been justified in initiating the fight. He continued wherever possible to discourage the opening of more liquor outlets that promoted alcoholism among the loggers.

Antle never hesitated to publish a joke on himself for the entertainment of loggers who read his magazine, humanizing the ecclesiastical image that might set him apart from them. At White Rock Bay, he wrote, he tried to get ashore by walking along the slippery boomsticks, lost his balance as his foot slipped, and fell headlong into the "salt chuck", causing great hilarity among the onlookers. Slapstick humour appealed to the loggers, and over the years the number of unfortunate clergymen who fell from booms and boats gave them plenty of amusement. That same day, at Lund, Antle wrote, he noticed on the wharf a man named George Hodgson. Due to an erroneous report, Hodgson's death had been written up in the previous month's *Log*. Hodgson looked exceptionally hale and hearty, and Antle produced a copy of the magazine for him, so he could enjoy the unusual experience of reading his own obituary.

At sea, however, navigation was a serious business; the ship came first, and humour, hospitality and even prayer were shelved when quick action was needed to run her efficiently. The Reverend Cyril Venables asked the captain to conduct a service in Venables' Vancouver church and was deeply impressed by his dignity and devoutness. In turn, Venables was asked to travel as guest on one of the *Columbia*'s trips. During a difficult docking in rough weather, the guest was astounded to be ordered about "like a dog" along with the rest of the crew, laggards receiving the rough edge of Antle's tongue.

This practical side of the chaplain's nature was illustrated by a perilous experience during an emergency run to Cape Scott, reported briefly in the *Daily News Advertiser* of February 26, 1909, and in more detail in Antle's Memoirs. A few miles off the cape the *Columbia*'s engines rattled to a stop. Great rollers were coming in from the sea, but they set their auxiliary sails and got the ship into a creek, securing her in a pool just big enough to float her. Then they rowed to Fisherman's Cove and walked four miles to the home of the patient. In a disused mill they found tools to fix the *Columbia*'s stripped gears, but the return trip to the vessel had still to be undertaken by rowboat. As they proceeded, their pilot rowing the forward set of oars and Antle operating the after set, Antle pointed out that the water was shoaling and the sea lifting, a warning of danger that he recognized from his Newfoundland days.

The pilot showed no concern, until suddenly the wave

John Antle. (Courtesy Mrs. F. Mennis)

The first *Columbia*. (Courtesy *Provincial Archives, Victoria*)

Dr. W.A.B. Hutton, first ship's doctor of Columbia Coast Mission. (*Courtesy C.G. Tuck*)

Dr. Daril Hannington and nurses Sutherland and Franklin at Queen's Hospital, Rock Bay, 1907. (*Courtesy C.G. Tuck*)

The Rev. John Antle and Mrs. Antle in the *Laverock* c. 1903. (*Courtesy Vancouver School of Theology*)

Queen's Hospital, Rock Bay, built in 1905. (*Courtesy Vancouver School of Theology*)

St. Michael's Hospital, Rock Bay, built in 1911 to replace Queen's Hospital which burned in 1910. (*Courtesy Vancouver School of Theology*)

The launching of the second *Columbia* in July 1910. (*Courtesy Vancouver School of Theology*)

The second *Columbia*. (*Courtesy Vancouver School of Theology*)

Taking the raft to school, Echo Bay. (*Courtesy Rev. P. Ellis*)

The *Eirene*, Squirrel Cove, August 2, 1911. (*Courtesy C.G. Tuck*)

John Antle and crew on second
Columbia, c. 1910. (*Courtesy
C.G. Tuck*)

Columbia Hospital, Texada
Island, opened 1907. (*Courtesy C.G. Tuck*)

Rev. Alan Greene aboard the
*Rendezvous, 1927. (Courtesy
Derek Lukin Johnston*)

First St. George's Hospital, Alert Bay, built in 1909. Burned down in 1923. (*Courtesy Vancouver School of Theology*)

The *Makehewi*, c. 1920. (*Courtesy Vancouver School of Theology*)

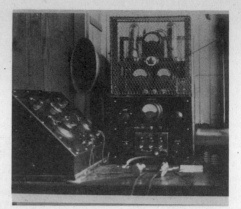

The first Whaletown church and hall, built in 1920. (*Courtesy C. G. Tuck*)

Marconi radio-telephone on second *Columbia*, 1927, one of the earliest on the coast for such boats. (*Courtesy Cecil Fitzgerald*)

C.H. Fitzgerald, Cecil Fitzgerald, Rev. John Antle, Tony Katsumato, aboard second *Columbia*, c. 1925. (*Courtesy Cecil Fitzgerald*)

Rev. John Antle accepting money from Indian chiefs at Village Island for an x-ray machine for St. George's Hospital, Alert Bay,
1925. (*Courtesy Cecil Fitzgerald*)

The Leask brothers, Bute Inlet, 1927. (*Courtesy Derek Lukin Johnston*)

Patient being hoisted aboard *Columbia*, c. 1929. Tony Katsumato at left. (*Courtesy Vancouver School of Theology*)

Floating hospital at O'Brien Bay. It was wrecked in a Johnstone Strait storm while being towed to Pender Harbour. (*Courtesy Vancouver School of Theology*)

ahead broke with a terrific roar and they were forced to back water furiously to escape annihilation. The pilot was weak with fright and acknowledged he had lost his bearings in the rising mist. He was unsure which rocks had caused the breaker. Antle took charge, rowed far out to sea, continued parallel to the shore, and finally headed in blindly for the creek through the darkness and mist. "If we hit bottom, every man for himself... swim towards the land and God help you," he said.

At this point his cook-engineer remembered his early religious training as son of a Methodist minister. "I haven't said my prayers for years," he quavered. "This seems to be the time to start again."

"It's hardly playing square with the Lord to wait until you're in a mess like this," Antle retorted. "Your present job is to keep water out of the boat, so bail!"

During his voyage in the *Laverock* in 1904, Antle had felt the urgent need for a hospital in Alert Bay on Cormorant Island. Without medical care, the health of the Indians had deteriorated alarmingly, as Antle had stated in his annual report of 1907. The following year the Indian Agent, William Halliday, held a meeting in Alert Bay at which he urged Antle to build a hospital for the Indian and white population. B.C. Packers, which ran a cannery there, would provide a free, one-acre site and $300 was offered as a start towards the project. Antle took up the challenge at once and went east to lecture and canvass, raising the necessary $5500 by his vigorous campaign. On June 15, 1909, Bishop Perrin travelled north again, this time to dedicate St. George's Hospital in Alert Bay. Dr. M.D. Baker was the first doctor, Miss Caroline Monk the matron and Miss Mary Motherwell the first nurse.

The bishop was kept busy dedicating hospitals, and John Antle raising money to build them. Queen's Hospital at Rock Bay burned down in 1910 and a 25-bed hospital with more modern equipment replaced it in 1911, Bishop Perrin performing the dedication ceremony. The new hospital received a new name: St. Michael's. [13]

Chapter Two

The Fleet Expands

I

In between raising money for hospitals, Antle turned his energies to campaigning for a new ship to replace the *Columbia*. Not only were her quarters cramped but also her low speed of seven knots was not powerful enough to combat northern storms and tides. In the fall of 1908, Antle travelled to England to look over suitable vessels. None were exactly right for his purpose, and he began a drive to raise money to build a new ship. Once again his intense conviction and persistence brought results.

His interview with Lord Strathcona, the Canadian High Commissioner, was typical. Antle chose him because he had donated two ships to the Grenfell Mission. However, he was greeted by the flat statement that Strathcona knew all about the Columbia Coast Mission and had decided not to give a penny towards the new ship. Antle attempted to describe the work, but Strathcona interrupted him impatiently to say he did not approve of Canadians coming to collect the pence of the English poor to build their institutions. This spark set off Antle, who leapt to his feet, exclaiming, "I'm not coming to the poor of England but to the rich of England . . . I'm coming to you, Lord Strathcona!"

38

The High Commissioner voiced an objection to Canadian missionaries who came to England and gave the impression that there were no schools, churches or hospitals when "we spend thousands of pounds advertising Canada and assuring people they will find these schools and churches when they go to Canada."

"Then you should not do it," declared Antle.

"Why not?"

"Because it's not true!" In his fervour, Antle advanced on Strathcona, who backed away instinctively from this impassioned zealot until he was cornered by the fireplace. "You send thousands of people to settle in isolated areas where there are no schools and churches," Antle cried, "and if it were not for us missionary beggars as you call us, there would be none of these services."

The commissioner pulled out a letter file from a table drawer and displayed a thick pile of letters: "All begging letters from institutions equally important as your own."

Undaunted, Antle demanded, "Is it a fair question to ask you how many you have replied to favourably?"

There was the usual long pause of shocked silence that greeted Antle's temerity, and then Strathcona capitulated. "You have the courage of your convictions anyway," he said, "and I'll give you five hundred pounds." He followed with interest the building of the second *Columbia*, and wished Antle Godspeed when he left England.

Antle continued his campaigning, in England and in Canada, sometimes meeting rebuffs but never faltering until the necessary funds were raised. He had brought from England the plans of the beautiful ship *Queen Margaret* that he saw berthed in Ireland, and designed the interior himself with the assistance of ship designer E. Trist. Sam Dawe of New Westminster was given the contract, and after many delays the ship was launched in New Westminster early in July 1910, from the ways of the Westminster Marine Railway Company.

The first *Columbia* was sold in 1910 and re-registered as *Chaos*. In 1914 she was sold to Harry Morgan of Victoria, and later was owned by Frank Cvitanovich and Jack Fiomengo of

Vancouver. Archdeacon Pentreath conducted the service for the new mission ship, which received the name of her predecessor, *Columbia*. Mrs. John Antle christened the ship, with genuine champagne this time, and the *Columbia* slid down the ways, her successful launching witnessed by several hundred spectators who were led in the hymn "For Those in Peril on the Sea" by the combined choirs of Holy Trinity Cathedral and St. Barnabas.

During the many delays in construction, Bishop A.U. de Pencier inspected the progress made, and bet Antle a silk hat that the ship would not be ready by the end of July, the date Antle had set. On July 31 the bishop was present at a reception on board the second *Columbia* and was reminded of the bet. Antle received his silk hat.

Overall measurements of the second *Columbia* were 100 by 17 feet, with a depth of 7.1 feet. Staffing her were skipper, doctor, engineer, deckhand and cook. Forward of her main deck was the main cabin, about 17 feet square, to be "luxuriously upholstered in red velvet" raptly predicted the Westminster *Daily News*, though the only red velvet was on the altar (the original altar from the first *Columbia*) and concealed when it was folded shut. The cabin (with upholstery in black leather) could hold up to 40 persons, though considerably more were crowded in for Christmas parties and moving picture shows. Here, during the 45 long years of her service with the mission, were held the baptisms, marriage ceremonies, Christmas concerts and church services that made the second *Columbia* a loved and long-remembered part of the lives of thousands of residents on the British Columbia coast. The cabin was even a court of justice at times, for Antle had become a justice of the peace. And from her decks, to complete the cycle, there were held many services for burial at sea.

The *Columbia* had a spacious deckhouse and a small but well-equipped hospital with dispensary and x-ray machine. Her diesel engine was later replaced by a 140-h.p. Atlas diesel which, said Antle, "contributed in a large way to the *Columbia*'s final success." The little mess room contained a table for four, though double the number sometimes gathered around it.

There was considerable criticism regarding both the size of the new *Columbia*, which many felt was needlessly large, and the practice of Antle and succeeding superintendents of entertaining visiting royalty and important clerical and lay dignitaries on board, which was considered unsuitable for a missionary ship. Some cited the early missionaries of various denominations who had travelled the coastal waters in dugout canoes, fittingly humble. But Antle was preparing for future years and an expansion which he expected and would work towards. He knew only too well that the raising of funds for upkeep of ships and hospitals was a fact of life he must constantly face, and with the publicity and resultant interest engendered by illustrious guests, the entertaining had its practical side.

Bishop de Pencier was one of the critics, calling the *Columbia* "a white elephant", but he changed his mind on one of the *Columbia*'s early runs. He had been told by his doctor to take a rest, and chose a trip on the *Columbia* for a relaxing holiday. The hospital room was converted into a stateroom for the bishop, and all went well despite strong winds until they reached Hardy Bay and prepared to cross the notoriously wild waters of Queen Charlotte Sound to Blunden Bay. The bishop had retired early, hoping for restful sleep, but during the crossing, which took three hours, double the normal time, agonized groans could be heard from the hospital room with each lurch and roll of the ship. Suddenly the *Columbia* gave a frightful heave, there was a crash as the legs of the bishop's bed collapsed, and he was tossed across the narrow room from one hospital bed right into the other.

When shelter was reached at last, guest and crew gathered around the mess table for a late repast, everyone too weary to talk. But Bishop de Pencier finally broke the silence with, "Well, Antle, I used to say this vessel was too big."

"Yes, you called her a white elephant," Antle reminded him austerely.

"I'm ready to take it all back now," said the suffering bishop. "I say she is too small!"

2

Alan Greene, a young student at Wycliffe College in Toronto, was asked in 1911 to come to British Columbia to work with the Columbia Coast Mission during his five months' summer vacation. The invitation came from the Reverend C.C. Owen of Christ Church in Vancouver who had known Alan's father, Canon R.W.E. Greene, a keen yachtsman and amateur boat builder. A character in Stephen Leacock's *Sunshine Sketches of a Little Town* is said to be based on Canon Greene, and Mariposa, the little town, is recognizable as Orillia, Ontario, Alan Greene's birthplace. Owen was sure the canon's son would be an excellent seaman as well, though the youth's experience consisted of summers as deckhand and purser on Great Lakes vessels during his school vacations, and sailing with his brother Heber aboard their father's boats on Lake Couchiching.

Young Greene jumped at the chance of what seemed to him a taste of danger and adventure in his chosen field. He knew nothing of gas-boats or the tides and rapids that complicate west-coast sea travel, but a friend showed him how to start an outboard engine and he hoped to balance inexperience with enthusiasm. John Antle, introduced to him at the mission office, gave him a quizzical look but promised to spend a week or so on board with him and reveal the mysteries of tides, charts and engines. Antle was comforted by the thought that the student would be no expense to the mission: Christ Church would pay his salary of $25 a month and supply his food as well as fuel for the *Eirene*, loaned for the summer by J.C. Keith.

The *Eirene*, named for the Greek goddess of peace, was a 30-foot craft with a temperamental, 10-h.p. gas engine. Greene experienced his first rough weather as Antle took her through the narrows and headed up the coast. Passing Bowen Island, the engine spluttered to a stop and they were nearly swept onto the rocks before Antle got her going, partly with the aid of a matchstick inserted in some vital area. They rested overnight at Snug Harbour and reached Van Anda the next afternoon, bucking a westerly all the way. Here, Antle discovered a Union steamship would be departing for Vancouver that night, and to young Greene's dismay he bade him farewell, leaving him with no instruction about tides or engines, and with the sole advice, "If you keep travelling, you'll find small logging camps all over the map. You'll just have to explore and find them. They're a pretty tough proposition when it comes to religion, and I don't know how you'll get along. But that's up to you."

Greene, feeling like a child whose parent throws him into the water, shouting "Sink or swim!", tied up the *Eirene* at Marble Bay for the night. His neighbour was a surly man who spoke neither to Greene nor to any of the other boatmen. These referred to him as "The Pirate" because of his fierce expression. A few years later when Greene returned to the mission as Antle's deckhand and chaplain on the *Columbia*, he asked the local sawmill owner at Van Anda about The Pirate. "Oh, he was hung for murder shortly after you left here," was the reply. "He had killed a policeman during a store robbery in Parksville two years before."

The nurses in Van Anda's Columbia Hospital, short of staff, taught the student missionary to help them as an anaesthetist when he was in port. Greene's love of slapstick comedy and practical jokes was apparent even in those days. He was told he could sleep in the hospital whenever he wished, but one night when he came in, there were no beds available in the private ward. There were three beds in the men's ward and only one of them was in use, but it was occupied by the corpse of a Mr. De Greek. The dead man lay in the far corner of the room, covered with a sheet. Several miners were expected at the hospital at midnight after finishing their shift, to measure the corpse for the coffin they were to construct up at the mine.

Greene was quite willing to share a room with a corpse. It was a perfect set-up. He lay down in a bed close to the door and covered himself completely with a sheet. A little after midnight he heard the men come quietly down the hall and open the door.

"There he is, just inside the door," said one. They had brought along a six-foot rod and this was laid gingerly over the top of the silent, sheeted form. "They said he was a six-footer," Greene heard. "He's nowhere near that. They were wrong."

The sheeted figure sat up in bed. "No, brother, you are wrong," it pronounced in sepulchral tones. "You've measured the wrong corpse."

There was a stampede for the door and the men tore down the hall in a panic. Greene hopped out of bed and pursued them to explain the joke. Still shocked and shaking, none of them saw the humour of it and the student chaplain had to listen to very forceful remarks regarding their opinion of him. For some time he was highly unpopular in Van Anda.

Antle, the Newfoundlander who had earned his captain's papers on a sea-going tug, was always skeptical of the abilities of clergy from Ontario and impatient if inept crew hampered his progress, but his parting words to Greene served as a challenge to the inexperienced student. Greene decided to start his preaching immediately at a logging camp at Grief Point, just south of Powell River. He crossed Malaspina Strait, tied up to a boom of logs and walked up to the camp to ask the foreman if he could hold a service for the loggers. "I don't give a damn what you do," replied the foreman, "but don't give my boys any sky dope. Keep to this life, not the next."

Greene went around among the men before supper and announced his service. He had hoped to pave the way during the meal, but a large sign, NO TALKING, kept him quiet, and to his dismay, the moment the men had wolfed their food in silence there was a general exodus from the camp of every man except the cooks, who had to clear up and go to bed early, and one man with a bad cut in his foot who was forced to stay. Greene did his best to entertain his congregation of one, but left for Powell River at five the next morning feeling like an actor whose first night was a ghastly failure.

Though differing in many ways from Antle, Greene had much of the first superintendent's persistence, and in Powell

River he regained his confidence by gathering together in the cookhouse a congregation of a respectable size. A little later, he took a logger from the hospital at Van Anda back to his camp at Lund in the *Eirene*; in gratitude the logger rounded up a few men to join the women Greene had collected from the wharf where they were waiting for the arrival of the steamer. The big loggers, most of them suffering from Saturday night hangovers, squeezed themselves into the small seats in the schoolroom.

After the service, Greene asked one of them to take up a collection, which he did, shaking his cap under the nose of each logger and demanding, "Cough up!" When he came back to Greene, looking at the modest contributions he asked, "Well, will I put her around again, old sport?" but Greene felt that once was all that his congregation could stand.

He had one embarrassing experience with the *Eirene* that year when he attempted to anchor at Manson's Landing on Cortes. Entering the lagoon, he was unaware of the telephone line stretched across the narrow entrance and tore it down with the *Eirene*'s mast, cutting off Campbell River from the mainland until the company restrung the lines, this time on higher poles.

Greene returned as a permanent member of the mission in 1912, serving the Squamish Valley and Britannia Mines and running up as far as Gibson's Landing in the *Eirene*. He raised several hundred dollars for a new church in Squamish, where Mr. Moody, mine superintendent of Britannia Mines, regarded him at first with some suspicion, since a pseudo-parson had recently come into the camp and proved to be a labour agitator in disguise. But Greene was accepted in time, and baptized Moody's little daughter as well as the children of the Graftons, lighthouse keepers at Point Atkinson.

In 1913, as ordained priest, Greene worked with Channel Hepburn, covering Campbell River and Quathiaski Cove. The *Columbia* was tied up at the International logging dump up the river that summer and served as a hospital for Campbell River residents before their hospital was built in 1914. On their first Sunday, Greene drew a congregation of three, while

Hepburn found one man willing to hear his sermon in Heriot Bay. Hepburn and his congregation of one climbed through a window in the Heriot Bay school and "joined in corporate worship." After this, they held a conference on the *Columbia* and decided two missionaries in the district were one too many. Greene took off for Whaletown on Cortes Island in a 14-foot, open gas-boat, his headquarters a little cabin overlooking the harbour. He marvelled, looking back in later years, that he survived his voyages in that little open boat through the Yaculta Rapids, Greene Point Rapids and the tide-rips around Salmon River as he visited logging camps and settlers on his tours of duty.

He ran in under shelter of any point offering protection when westerlies caught him at sea. Dropping anchor, he would doze sitting up, so stiff and cold when he got back to his cabin at Whaletown that he had difficulty climbing out of the boat. When snow came, he was forced to take to the *Cassiar* and the Canadian Pacific's *Queen City*.

He also acted as deckhand and chaplain for Antle on the *Columbia* around this time. According to Dan McGregor, an early engineer on the ship, Antle occasionally sent Greene ashore at some little village, instructing him to "give them a good service and make sure to bring back plenty of vegetables".[1] The amiable Greene, whose easy-going nature resulted in a certain amount of disorganization, found the complex character of his captain at once inspiring and intimidating. Antle's ideals and energy were inspiring; his banter and disparagement were discouraging to a beginner and his angry outbursts were disconcerting. The *Columbia* had tied up one time at the *Cardena*'s berth at the end of the float in Shoal Bay and was forced to move back when the Union Steamship vessel arrived. Instead of starting up the engine, Antle decided to haul the boat back manually with the help of young Greene. An offshore wind hampered them as Antle, forward, and Greene, aft, hauled at the ropes.

"Take in your slack!" Antle roared at Greene, who was heaving with all his strength. Greene pulled the rope taut but the wind was blowing the boat in the opposite direction with equal force.

"Take in that slack!" Antle roared again as the *Cardena* drew closer.

"There isn't any!" Greene shouted back desperately.

"Well, then," thundered Antle with a resounding oath, "make some!"

Along with his seamanship, John Antle had acquired a sailor's vocabulary. Tales of his salty language come from many of the crew. Engineer Cecil Fitzgerald remembers an occasion on the *Columbia* when the ship arrived at Turnbull Cove to find the harbour blocked by a log boom. Antle called out to the logger to release the centre logs to open up a passage, and got back a refusal peppered with profanity. Antle leapt to the bow of the *Columbia* and blasted the logger with a furious stream of oaths that electrified young Fitzgerald, who was standing nearby, and left him open-mouthed. The logger was evidently so startled to hear himself outsworn by a captain in a clerical collar that he moved his logs without further protest and the *Columbia* sailed serenely into port.

Antle may have damned those who crossed him, but he eschewed blasphemy and sought control of his fiery nature. In 1890, the year of his graduation from Queen's College, he was given a copy of Sadler's *Gospel according to St. Matthew, with notes critical and practical,* and a comment on oaths that he underlined reads: ". . . what He means seem entirely confined in their scope to . . . holy things profanely invoked." He underlined: ". . . the one thing needing . . . that we be able to show . . . that we have been merciful, loving, kind, sympathizing." Also marked are lines that expressed his working philosophy: "Not with the hope of gaining ought, nor seeking a reward . . ."

Top rank in any field never intimidated Antle, and he found it impossible to curb his ire if he thought his ships were treated with insufficient respect. The *Columbia* II was anchored in a coastal bay on one occasion when a navy vessel sailed in and anchored nearby. Almost immediately a boat was lowered and sped over to the *Columbia.* Pointing to the mission flag, the officer in charge shouted, "Take down that flag!"

Antle came on deck. "Why?" he demanded.

"You're flying a vice admiral's flag. The captain says get it down immediately!"

Antle's temper exploded. The Columbia Coast Mission's official flag, besides its red St. George's cross on a white ground, has a small red cross in the dexter canton (the upper corner nearest to the staff.) The vice admiral's flag is similar, except that instead of a small red cross it has a small red ball. At a distance the two might be confused. Antle's outraged blast seared the ears of his crew and sent the navy men back to their ship in a flurry to report the mistake to their embarrassed captain.

Another incident on the *Columbia* involved a European physician who was serving temporarily as ship's doctor in order to earn his Canadian certificate. He had brought on board with him a huge German Shepherd dog of uncertain temper that was usually kept tied up on the afterdeck but on this occasion for some reason had been let loose. John Antle had joined the ship on an inspection tour. Coming along the deck, he went to step up into the wheelhouse when the dog suddenly jumped at him from the rear and bit him. Antle's verbal response turned the air blue. Very shortly after this, doctor and dog left the ship.

It was enough to reinforce Antle's conviction that dogs had no place on a ship. Several of the chaplains were known to keep pets on board, however. Captain George MacDonald, who served for many years on the second *Columbia,* took his wife and their little dog Bingo aboard on some of his tours of duty during the summer months. Bingo was a gift from "Auchie", the ship's cook, and derived his name from the captain's habit of prefacing the climax to his stories with: "Then, bingo!" Seagulls drove Bingo wild; when they swooped over the ship he would hurtle down the deck in pursuit, eyes on the birds, and shoot overboard off the stern into the sea. The pike pole would be seized and Bingo fished out by his collar, half choked. Eventually the captain stipulated that a harness must replace the collar so Bingo could be hauled safely aboard.

Colonel Goodland, a member of the mission board who was a guest on a *Columbia* tour, speaks of the din set up by the Reverend Gilbert Thompson's little dog when they were anchored in Wakeman Sound off Kingcome Inlet and a cougar chased a deer down the mountain and into the water close to the ship. Alan Greene had a series of cocker spaniels that travelled with him in later days in the *Rendezvous*. Pep always stood in the bow as land neared, to be the first ashore. Patty fell overboard and was drowned, while the third spaniel brought Greene into conflict with the law when it took to chasing sheep. An irate rancher on Quadra Island shot the dog and found wool in its stomach. Greene was taken to court and in the face of such evidence was regretfully fined by a fellow missionary and justice of the peace, R.J. Walker.

Greene enjoyed with mischievous delight the rare occasion when he found his captain in the wrong. As the *Columbia* rounded Chatham Point, Greene remarked that he'd noticed in passing that the lighthouse oil tank under the light had been painted white instead of its former red. In his usual positive manner, Antle told him he was mistaken and deplored his frail powers of observation. Greene was moved to justify his conviction and bet $5 against a new fishing rod that he was right. As soon as they docked, he appealed to Big Mike, the Swedish wharfinger, who replied, "Oh, yah, dey haf yust painted her vite dis veek." Greene got his fishing rod, but hadn't the courage to mention frail powers of observation to his captain.

Antle erred once, to his considerable embarrassment, while endeavouring to do a good turn. Tugboat captain Wilfred (Bill) Dolmage tells the tale. "I remember talking to one of the most famous loggers, P.B. Anderson, who had a large logging show up coast. This is his story: In those days there were many charter boats running up the coast with girls aboard, supposedly hairdressers. Also they could put on a floor show, but their unadvertised services were pretty well known to the camps. The captain of one of these boats went over to the *Columbia*; he had heard that she was leaving the next day for up coast and asked the Rev. Antle if he would mind putting up notices that he would be arriving at the different camps a few days later. I am sure the Rev. Antle didn't realize what business this fellow was in until old P.B. saw him putting up the notice in his camp. He didn't put up any more."

Bill Dolmage adds a note about the second *Columbia*: "A lot of us who knew what a wonderful ship she was were sure upset when she was sold and called the *Wayward Lady*."

Antle enjoyed singing, and he and Greene sometimes harmonized in hymns as they plied the northern waters. Greene recorded on tape his happy memories of such times. At services, too, Antle would sing while Greene played the portable organ, but here Greene's ineptitude was apt to irritate the man who expected efficiency. "Why on earth don't you play the correct bass?" Antle demanded, and Greene explained that he couldn't read music and the bass was his own creation. "It certainly is," Antle commented severely. "You throw me all off." It is hard to meet the requirements of a perfectionist.

His standard of performance was set high for crew, and for his sons, according to his son Ernest Antle. Antle and his wife separated, with Mrs. Antle taking Marian and Antle assuming the care of his sons. Victor was sent to train on H.M.S. *Conway*, an old sailing ship used as a training vessel on the Mersey River in England. Ernest attended a school in Québec. Both boys spent their holidays with Antle as deckhands on the *Columbia*, earning $10 each per month. The boys were catechized daily on boxing the compass. This was before the compass card was marked in degrees instead of points, and Victor and Ernest learned to reel off the 32 points: N, N by E, NNE, NE by N and so on, until eventually they were familiar with all 128 points.

The boys were never allowed to take the wheel without supervision, but Ernest was once left aboard the *Columbia* as watchman when she was tied up to a bag boom of logs in Coal Harbour in Vancouver for a few days around 1914. During the night a gale started up, the boom broke loose from the piling, and boom and *Columbia* were blown out to the mouth of the harbour. Ernest, a youngster in his early teens, showed something of his father's ingenuity. He was unable to start the engine, but he managed to let go the locks to drop the anchors. The *Columbia*'s possible drift out into the stormy seas was arrested, and boom and ship stayed firmly at anchor until help arrived.

The *Columbia* was the mission's only active ship during World War I due to the shortage of doctors, clergy and crew, and the scarcity of gasoline. Other missions suspended their service for the duration of the war, but Antle continued to hold regular church services at 20 places along the coast as well as supplying medical and social help. He wrote in his superintendent's report of December 31, 1914: "Since October no other religious body has been working in the district and it has meant much to the settlers at a time when people are deeply stirred by unprecedented circumstances... in times of stress [the Columbia Coast Mission] was alone in the field bringing a message of comfort."

The start of the war brought on a depression which resulted in the closing down of almost all the camps at Rock Bay, a blow to the mission which depended largely on their support. St. Michael's Hospital was forced to cut its staff drastically. There was no doctor, and the nursing staff was reduced from three to two. By 1915 conditions were more stable in the logging field and Dr. C.T. McCallum was appointed to the hospital.

3

The war drew many of the clergy overseas to serve as chaplains. These included Bishop de Pencier, who left Archdeacon Heathcote to administer his diocese of New Westminster. Alan Greene, his brother Heber and Channel Hepburn were also among those who went overseas. When war broke out, Alan Greene was acting as curate in St. Paul's Church in Toronto. It was a comfortable city posting, involving attendance at social functions clad in formal attire. His top hat at such affairs was a dramatic contrast to the informal sailor's cap and Indian sweater of a sea-going, west-coast missionary. But as he watched a succession of young men called to battle, Greene felt impelled to follow them. He was urged to remain at his post, but in 1916 he gained his wish and became chaplain to the 10th Royal Grenadiers. It was assumed that he would return to Toronto when war ended, but instead he wrote to John Antle and arranged to rejoin the mission.

He had lived with men who faced death daily and he believed this had given him more understanding of loggers whose work involved constant danger and who in consequence lived in the present with little thought of the future. He had left the mission disheartened by the unproductive hours spent tinkering with recalcitrant engines and preaching to the unregenerate, but now he was inspired to try again. Friends in Toronto had helped to raise the money for a mission boat. He would skipper the *Makehewi*, his headquarters to be Quathiaski Cove on Quadra Island.

Quadra and Cortes Islands were growing in population. Earlier on, Quadra Island was served by Fred Comley, a lay missionary at the time, who conducted his services in the old Pidcock home. His little boat was the *Governor Musgrave*, named in 1911 after the last Royal Governor of British Columbia, who was in office from 1869 to 1871, the year of British Columbia's entry into Confederation. She was donated by his widow for missionary work and used by Comley, who also served in Van Anda and Alert Bay. Comley played a large part in obtaining in 1916 the first church of the mission, St. John's, at Quathiaski Cove, and employed his skill at building chimneys to construct them for several churches erected by the mission. Comley was ordained in later years, served on the mission board, and received the title of canon.

Greene settled in Quathiaski Cove, in charge of St. John's Church, and in 1920 began his four years of service on the *Makehewi*, first taking a honeymoon trip in her with his bride, Gertrude Finlayson, whom he had married in Toronto. One of the reasons that Alan Greene served so long with the mission (over 40 years) — apart from his dedication to his work, his vitality to carry it through and his love for his ships and the waters he came to know so intimately — was Gertrude Greene's willing acceptance of the difficult life of a west-coast missionary's wife.

Many of the young clergymen who came to the mission eager to serve were unprepared for the difficulties experienced by their wives, who left the contacts and amenities of city life to be alone for long periods in primitive surroundings, struggling to raise their children without the help of their sea-going husbands. The men served well, but their terms were short. Alan Greene had worked for the mission; he knew the hardships, and his honest descriptions of the life included these as well as the beauties and freedom of the coast. It took Gertrude several years to decide, but when she made up her mind at 29 (Greene was 30), she came ready to accept reality. An attractive young woman, much loved by all, she opted for a mundane life, raising five children on the island, performing the many duties of a pastor's wife, and remaining at home without complaint when Greene sailed away lightheartedly or flew east on his many campaigns.

The Reverend H.M. Bolton was Greene's first assistant but resigned the following year. However, Cecil Fitzgerald, who became his deckhand and engineer in 1923, stayed with the ships for 15 years: a year on the *Makehewi*, a year on the *Rendezvous* and over 12 years as deckhand and engineer on the *Columbia*. He edited *The Log* for five years and at present serves as a board member of the mission.

Fitzgerald says an old logger told him a long, involved story of how the *Makehewi* got her name, saying a Chinook princess was abducted by Haida raiders and when her lover tried to rescue her his canoe was swept on the rocks and smashed. The Makehewi bird took pity on the lovers, plucked the maiden from the Haida canoe and dropped her on the beach by her lover. The tribe thereafter revered the Makehewi bird as good, faithful and true, and thus *Makehewi* was a fit name for a missionary ship.

Fitzgerald printed this romantic version in *The Log*, but added that Mr. W.K. Sulley, son of the former owner, had quashed the theory by explaining to Fitzgerald that the name was a scrambled combination of the first letters of names of two of the owner's children, Helen Marjorie and William Kenneth (Mr. W.K. Sulley being William Kenneth and thus a good authority.) Sulley said his father found the old boat beached and abandoned in the mud in Bremerton. He brought her up and had her refitted in Port Blakely,

Washington, as a pleasure boat, registering her under her new name in 1910. She was sold to the mission on October 6, 1920, and registered January 13, 1921.

When Cecil Fitzgerald was engineer, the 35-foot vessel had a huge, two-cylinder Union engine that burned a foul-smelling distillate and was sparked by a primitive make-and-break system. Starting her required a combination of scientific skill and brute strength. The operator, Fitzgerald says, "needed the strength of an ox and the agility of a kangaroo to roll the massive flywheel by hand and leap for the half compression levers and titillate the carburetor."

The *Makehewi* had Bishop Schofield aboard on one trip through Seymour Narrows, and her engine stalled as she hit the big waves surging over Ripple Rock. For a half hour she wallowed in a westerly tide rip as Fitzgerald struggled with the baulky engine. It was always a subtle satisfaction to the chaplains of the mission boats when one of the "big shots" was given a taste of the discomforts endured by the coast missionaries, but in this case the bishop braced himself at each lurch of the ship and refused to be seasick.

The *Columbia* covered the northern run and the *Makehewi* ran between Quathiaski and Sayward. Ports of call varied with weather conditions and the shifting of logging camp locations. During 1922 the *Columbia* was tied up for repairs and the *Makehewi* took over both routes, logging roughly 5000 miles. She had her share of drama. She was anchored at Alert Bay one night, preparatory to heading the next morning for Kingcome Inlet, when Dr. Wilson, the hospital doctor, came aboard to say a woman from a Thompson Sound logging camp had arrived at the hospital as a maternity patient. The doctor's wife had taken in the patient's four children during the delivery, and now was sheltering the mother and new baby as well, there being no lodging available in Alert Bay. The children were wrecking the furniture and the nerves of Mrs. Wilson, and the doctor entreated Greene to take the family back to Thompson Sound.

Greene took them aboard, along with a convalescent logger also waiting for transportation. The *Makehewi* got to the small logging camp by afternoon, only to find that the father of the family had gone to Vancouver, taking with him all the furniture, including stove and beds. The mother and her five offspring crowded onto the *Makehewi* again and shelter for them was sought on Minstrel Island, where the Hoods agreed to put them up for the night. At six a.m. the *Makehewi* began her return trip to Alert Bay, wondering if the family was to be a permanent fixture on the ship. The crossing was very rough this time, and all the children were sick in pails provided by the crew. Fortunately, the cannery manager at Alert Bay rose to the occasion and took in the six homeless wanderers until police could locate the father.

Another time, Sidney Marshall, the policeman at Quathiaski Cove, asked Greene to take him in the *Makehewi* to Okisollo Channel to bring down the body of a woman who was an accident victim. She and her husband had come from England to settle on the coast and had been living in a rough little shack half buried among bracken, devil's club and alder. The husband was away, working as an oiler on a tug in an effort to make ends meet, when the Englishwoman rowed over to a neighbour's cabin to ask if her mail could be picked up at Waiatt Bay. Returning home, she slipped and fell off her rickety float, hit her head as she fell and drowned in six feet of water.

The neighbour, coming later with the mail, carried her to the shack, built a rough coffin of cedar shakes and went to phone the only policeman for the area. There was no radio-telephone on boats then, and after the return from Okisollo to Quathiaski on the *Makehewi*, Marshall contacted the tug company, which sent one of their larger tugs to search the straits for the husband. Eventually his tug was found in Welcome Pass, and he was brought down to Quathiaski and then to Vancouver. Here the wife, who had been an army nurse in World War I, was buried in the soldiers' plot. The bereaved husband committed suicide soon after this.

It was to families such as these, struggling to survive, and alone for long periods in the bush, that the mission boats strove to bring medical, spiritual and social comfort. Knowledge that the mission boats would check on them periodically and were ready to answer any emergency call was reassuring to these isolated settlers. One upcoast resident wrote to *The Log*: "... we have the comfortable feeling that if we had an emergency she would be here as soon as called to do all possible ... we can never thank them enough for all they have done for us."[2]

The Anglican Church was also anxious to establish centres of worship, and in the 1920s churches were built on Cortes Island at Whaletown, Manson's Landing and Squirrel Cove. It meant that Antle and Greene were forced to campaign more strenuously than ever, now that funds from donations were spread thinner, in order to build and support churches as well as ships and hospitals. They rejoiced in the churches, but wished that support was not diverted from their own costly enterprise.

In September 1920, Columbia Hospital at Van Anda on Texada Island was closed permanently, due to exhaustion of the Tacoma Steel Company's copper mine on the island. Originally a dance hall, the building had been taken over by the Columbia Coast Mission in 1907 at the request of the mining company for a hospital for their workers at the site of their mine.

4

The first St. George's Hospital at Alert Bay burned down on August 18, 1923, and Antle immediately set about raising money to replace it with a larger and better-equipped building. On May 13, 1925, the hospital was formally opened by Major Selden Humphreys, DSO, ADC, representing the Lieutenant-Governor. The *Columbia* arrived with Antle piloting her, and carrying Bishop Schofield, who dedicated the hospital, and Archdeacon Heathcote.

One hundred cadets of the Indian industrial school, girls of the Indian Girls' Home and the Indian saxophone band welcomed them ashore, where Welcome and *Hamatsa* dances were performed for them by the Indians. Chief Whonnock of Fort Rupert said in his speech, "This hospital is to us the house of salvation and the house of hope. Salvation for the present and hope for the generations to come."

Later, the *Columbia* called at reserves at Village Island and Alert Bay where, after long speeches by Antle and by the Indians, sacks of money totalling $1500 were presented to Antle. The money, a large sum for those days, was donated for an x-ray machine for the hospital. The Indians felt this was their special institution. Indians and whites were in separate wards, but the mission went to great lengths to give equal service to both, and allowances were made for Indian families to visit patients at all hours, respecting the Indian patients' desire to have family nearby during illness. Thus the *Columbia* would often bring in a boatload of relatives and their belongings as well as an Indian patient from some remote village. Other relatives in Alert Bay took in the visitors, and the patient, relaxed and reassured, was surrounded by familiar faces. The hospital informality during the years of mission administration was something the Indians missed when the government took over and strict regulations were enforced.

The *Makehewi* proved inadequate; she was sold in 1924 to Betram O. Pinder of Vancouver. In 1927 she was registered to Thomas Campbell, her foreign name listed as *Charlotte S.* The mission replaced her on March 7, 1924, with the *Rendezvous*, built that year by Hoffar Motor Boat Company in Vancouver. While the ship was being readied, Alan Greene decided on her name as he was travelling south on the *Makehewi*. Fitzgerald was at the wheel, and Greene was in the cabin struggling to get out his monthly report, typing painfully in the hunt-and-peck manner.

"Where are we now?" Greene shouted to Fitzgerald.

"Just passing the Rendezvous Islands," his engineer called back.

The typing ceased, and Greene was heard muttering, "Rendezvous...Rendezvous..." Then, "I've got it!" he exclaimed. "*Rendezvous* is a good name for the ship. It suggests the islands we pass and the visits we make to the islanders."

The typing recommenced with vigour as Greene set down his recommendation for the name of the new vessel.

The *Rendezvous*, a 31-foot cabin cruiser with four-cylinder engine, could be handled in a pinch by one man in all but the worst storms. Her seven-by-12-foot cabin could seat 12 and was large enough for small church services, and many baptisms and communion services were held on board for settlers who rejoiced in this place of worship resembling in miniature the churches they had left behind them in the cities. But Greene and Fitzgerald often rowed ashore and packed portable organ and moving picture apparatus through the bush to camps. These inducements always lured a little gathering, usually to the bunkhouse or schoolhouse, but the services that prefaced the entertainment were important to many as well.

Alan Greene recalled one winter day up the coast when he called with the *Rendezvous* at a lonely cabin made of poles and cedar shakes. The father of the family, just out from England, had drowned when he fell through the ice on an island lake. A homesteader with a boy of 13 had taken in the widow and her young child; no one else offered aid, unwilling to brave the cold, stormy weather. The homesteader dug a grave on a small point overlooking a view of which the father had been fond. Greene and the boy got the coffin down to the shore and into a dugout canoe, which they towed behind their rowboat. As they rowed, they had to pause often to break the ice that had formed near the shore. Then there was an arduous journey up the hillside to the grave among the trees where the homesteader and the woman with her child were waiting. It was a sad little ceremony, marking an end to the immigrants' hopeful plans, a scene enacted all too often in those remote areas.

Calls on parishioners along the coast required a pastor able to adapt himself to a very varied congregation. Greene sat talking to a man in a little cabin one day when loud sounds like rifle fire made him jump to his feet. The reports came from below the cabin floor, but the man, to reassure him, lifted a trap door and showed him rows of bottles. Wine had fermented in them, and the corks were shooting out with the unnerving sound of gunfire.

The chaplain always enjoyed a visit to the Thompson family on the Rendezvous Islands. Thompson was one-armed, but he logged, fished, boated and farmed and had built his own house. As the *Rendezvous* approached the landing, Greene would blow the ship's whistle; this was the signal for Mrs. Thompson to line up her children in a row, seated in rocking chairs of varying size according to the age of the child. It was, apparently, her method of keeping them quietly occupied when guests arrived. They all rocked happily and rhythmically throughout Greene's visit, and the chaplain found his body rocking irresistibly in a corresponding rhythm as he went down the line shaking hands with each child in turn.

Funerals were often unconventional. Greene was asked by an undertaker to officiate at the burial of a man named Tompkins who drowned in Discovery Passage and was washed up in Duncan Bay. He went to Campbell River in the *Rendezvous* and was met by the undertaker in a 1920 Ford. They went first to the Willows Hotel where the undertaker hoped to round up some helpers. A husky logger agreed to lend a hand and roped in several of his pals as well. At the mortuary, the logger, a born organizer, hailed a passing truck to transport the coffin, and the undertaker led the way in his Ford to an old logged-off area. Somewhere off the very bad road the grave was waiting, he said, already dug.

There was a hunt, first to find the trail and then to find the grave. As the loggers heaved the coffin over one big deadfall, the forward handles pulled off and the men sat down backwards into devil's club and wild blackberry spikes, their colourful comments irreverent but understandable. The grave was found, the service held and the grave refilled. Then the big logger demanded a grave marker. There was none. He hunted about in the bushes, found an empty whisky bottle, wrote the dead man's name on a bit of paper and thrust it into the bottle, which he stuck neck down in the dirt of the grave. All being in order, Greene was driven to the wharf where the loggers waved him a farewell and headed for the hotel bar.

5

Lukin Johnston, a Vancouver journalist, sailed as a temporary crew member on the *Rendezvous* in 1926 with Alan Greene; also along was his 14-year-old son Derek who acted as a cabin boy during school holidays. Derek, a tall youngster plagued by adolescent clumsiness, had managed to break an amazing number of items on the boat the previous summer, including the glass skylight through which he accidentally thrust his head. His father presented Greene with five dollars at the start of this trip to pay for damages the ship was certain to suffer. Forty years later Derek, by then a sedate member of the mission board, asked Greene to officiate at his son's wedding. Greene's letter of acceptance contained one of the cartoons he delighted to draw, this one showing Derek's head crashing through the skylight of the *Rendezvous*.

Lukin Johnston recorded his impressions in articles in the Vancouver *Province, The Log*, and in a chapter of his book of travels, *Beyond the Rockies*. At first hand, he saw the people served by the ambulance ship as they searched out settlers in remote bays and inlets. Often the woman of the family was alone, doing a man's work tending to animals and developing their little farm while the husband was away in a logging camp. With no school nearby, the task of educating the children also fell to the mother.

In one such isolated spot, up Pendrell Sound, which almost bisects Redonda Island, a woman lay very ill in a handlogger's shack that could only be reached by crossing a boom of slippery logs. The logger dared not attempt the crossing to his boat while carrying the suffering woman. As so often happened, the *Rendezvous* rounded the point in the nick of time, sounding a welcome siren that brought the man to his door. A stretcher was quickly improvised by tearing off the door of the shack, and logger and ship's crew, slipping and sliding over the wet logs that heaved in the swell, carried the patient to the *Rendezvous* and got her to the hospital in time for a successful operation for acute appendicitis.

The *Rendezvous* continued on to Refuge Cove on West

Redonda for a scheduled service in the schoolhouse, a building no longer in use as a school due to a lack of pupils. Several rowboats arrived on time, and three or four adults and a number of children assembled to sing hymns to the music of the portable organ, to listen to a simple service and to spend some time exchanging news before rowing back to their scattered homes.

Lukin Johnston remarked on the unique service of the Columbia Coast Mission. "There are several missions working among these islands, doing splendid work," he wrote, "but of them all the Columbia Coast Mission is the largest. . . . Mission work of this kind is unlike any other kind of ministerial work in many respects . . . 'preaching' is a minor matter. Services are held, of course, on Sundays at more or less regular intervals, but they are of the simplest character. Questions of doctrine do not worry these isolated settlers very much. Over and over again they have found the sky pilot to be a 'very present help in time of trouble' and they have come to look on him, not so much as a preacher, but rather as an exponent of eminently practical Christianity."[3]

Other visits to a lonely spot in Pendrell Sound were made to George Pendrell and to the Otto Ellingsens. In the evening, the Emory and Ellingsen families came on board the *Rendezvous*, the organ was unfolded, song sheets were distributed, and the group sang blithely, ending with hymns and a prayer by the padre. Settlers remembering those days say the very fact that the boats called on them was heartening and encouraging, assuring them they were not forgotten.

Alan Greene kept a little notebook in which he wrote down messages to carry from one stop to another, or information, perhaps about a boy whose parents worried about his welfare. Greene would look up the boy, keep in touch, and reassure the family when he called again.

There were surprises on the tour. They were cruising up Bute Inlet one afternoon when a Bute wind blew up and they decided to search for a sheltered bay. Johnston was certain that no one would be living in so lonely an area, but Greene was not so sure. They came to a tiny bay and at one side of it saw several rough shacks. A huge log served as a wharf, and as they tied up to it and tooted the ship's whistle, an elderly man emerged and ran down to meet them, his face beaming a welcome.

They were climbing ashore when another oldster appeared, and still a third, all in their late 70s and all delighted to greet their visitors. They were the three bachelor Leask brothers who had come from the Scottish Orkney Islands and had lived contentedly for 12 years in this remote spot. Entering the shack, the guests were amazed to see the walls covered with shelves containing hundreds of books, including sets of Ruskin and Shakespeare. The shed behind the shack was filled with old magazines, including the *Atlantic Monthly*, which the old men preserved like priceless treasures.

Their soft Scottish voices and courteous manners made it less surprising to learn that the brothers had followed professions of banker, accountant and sea captain in former years. They exhibited the paintings of coastal scenes by Charles Leask, and telescope that Alfred Leask was making by hand in one of the sheds. They took the crew up the hill to see their roothouse, built of stone into the side of the hill, and their little sawmill run by a hand-made cedar water wheel, turned by water piped down from a lake. The guests were also shown a rowboat and oars that were being constructed. Behind the shacks stretched a garden and orchard and there were goats to provide milk for the enterprising trio.

Alan Greene found some recent editions of the *Atlantic Monthly* on board his boat, and the delighted brothers stood clutching these and waving farewell to the *Rendezvous* until it passed from their sight.

(Some ten years later the *Rendezvous* called again, with Doug Morton as Greene's engineer. Still cheerful and active, the octogenarians welcomed them and insisted they stay for a drink and snack. The old men were vegetarians, food faddists in Morton's view. The guests were served Ovaltine, no favourite with the engineer, and huge chunks of a sort of heavy, damp pudding filled with gigantic raisins. Greene swallowed his pudding manfully, but Morton chose a moment when he was unobserved to slip his portion into his pocket. After the visit, as they climbed aboard the *Rendez-vous,* Alan Greene groaned and clutched his stomach: "That was terrible. I feel sick." Doug said cheerfully: "I feel fine." Once out of sight of the brothers he had dropped his pudding into the salt chuck and only suffered from a very damp pocket.)

Up Homfray Channel, above Desolation Sound, the *Rendezvous* called at the Lindburg farm. Lukin Johnston was startled when they were met by the Lindburg brothers, two stalwart Swedes clad only in bright red bathing-suits and heavy boots and socks. This was their working garb all year round as they were firm believers in fresh air and sunshine. They grew vegetables and fruit trees, and their stock included goats, poultry, pigs and over a hundred turkeys which they raised for export from this remote spot. One of the brothers suddenly shouted out, "Queen! Queen!" and a little fawn came bounding from a shed. It had been orphaned when a cougar killed its mother and was quite tame and unafraid of the men.

Many settlers were unable to cope as successfully as these hardy pioneers. Some who lived alone were struck by "cabin fever", the mental delusions induced by loneliness. Their rough shacks up the inlets, surrounded by forest and a sea empty of human passage, were fertile ground for the malady. Some were struck by a persecution mania and fired shots from their cabins at imaginary enemies. More than once Alan Greene was forced to brave gunfire before he could win a lonely hermit's confidence. Their living conditions were often found to be tragic, the bed a pile of branches and food reduced to berries or handouts from an occasional passer-by who earned their trust. The chaplain would leave food and other necessities with the hermits if they could not be persuaded to return to civilization for hospital care.

The *Rendezvous* called at intervals to check on one old man who lived alone in the woods and was determined to eschew all contacts with humanity. His cabin contained only one window, and this faced the forest; there was no window in the wall facing the sea and its occasional traffic. The hermit, who had grown a long beard and always wore an old derby hat indoors and out, had only a number of cats for company and these had grown wild and fierce. One day he was found drowned below Point Sarah, clutching a large rock to ensure that he would sink. Poverty was not his problem; he had over $100 in his pockets and the inside walls of his cabin were so thickly lined with unopened cans of food that Greene thought at first they were a built-in lining to the walls.

The *Rendezvous* upheld its reputation of appearing in time of need during Quadra Island's great fire of 1926. The flames, starting in the north at Granite Bay, had swept down as far as Gowlland Harbour in the southwest and were spreading across the narrow neck of land towards Heriot Bay. Author Francis Dickie and his wife Suzanne were preparing to abandon their newly-built house to the flames when the *Rendezvous* appeared from around the point, towing the Forestry boat with its fire-fighting apparatus. The *Rendezvous* had come upon the disabled boat and offered to tow it to Dickie's cliffside home. Using water pumped from the sea, the crew was able to hold back the flames and save the house.

6

The practice of hosting dignitaries on the *Columbia* often had profitable results. One trip that demonstrated graphically the need for more equipment on the ship was a special run to Quatsino Sound on Vancouver Island's west coast with Bishop Schofield, Dr. C. Wace, and a noted canon from England as guests. They all rose at four in the morning to be sure of getting around Cape Scott on the northern tip of Vancouver Island before dark, and reached Quatsino wharf at seven in the evening. As they docked, a man called to them from the balcony of a building that there had been a day-long search for the *Columbia*. The wife of one of the wireless operators at Bull Harbour on Hope Island was in serious condition from a severe hemorrhage. This was before wireless was added to the ship.

The *Columbia*'s doctor was not among the crew on this special trip, but Dr. Wace agreed to go with Antle on the back-tracking run to Bull Harbour. By the time they made their way out of Quatsino Sound to the Pacific it had grown dark, and fog and a heavy sea slowed them as they fought their way north and around Cape Scott to Bull Harbour. Only once did they glimpse land through the fog until they arrived about 2:30 in the morning. Antle had been on duty steadily since four o'clock the previous morning and his knees were buckling from the strain of standing so long at the wheel. He retired to his bunk to rest while the doctor went ashore to treat the patient. In the morning, with great difficulty, they were able to hoist the seriously ill woman aboard the *Columbia* and rush her to the Alert Bay hospital. Dr. Wace had a convincing story to tell of the need for wireless and for a stretcher with permanent hoisting slings, and funds for these were soon provided for the ship. About 1927, John Antle installed one of the earliest Marconi radio-telephones in service among boats of her kind on the coast.

Now the *Columbia* contacted the Alert Bay wireless station every hour on the hour daily to receive emergency calls. Camps that had wireless also made a call once a day to Alert Bay. Soon after the *Columbia*'s radio-telephone had been installed, a call came from Alert Bay to pick up a logger who had been badly injured when a big tree rolled over him. It would be a 50-mile trip, and Antle estimated it would take him three hours. When they arrived, the foreman said sternly, "You're three minutes late." "What, is the man dead?" Antle asked in alarm. "No, but I heard you say on the wireless you'd be here in three hours," the foreman grinned.

Letters to *The Log* show the deep appreciation of isolated settlers for the visits of the *Columbia* and for the wireless telephone that brought her quickly in emergencies. One letter[4] in 1930 was from Mrs. Wright, wife of the Fisheries guardian who lived with her husband and four-year-old boy in a float house off George Point in Grappler Sound, above Sullivan Bay. "We had few visitors and trips of the *Columbia* were anticipated with joy," she says. One day the little family set out for Embley Lagoon in their gas-boat, the child sitting alone in the bow. His parents called him to come to them in the stern, and as he passed the engine he slipped, his clothes caught in the propeller shaft and before the father could stop the engine the boy's leg was pulled down below the engine's shafts and badly mangled. The muscles were torn off, and the engine's revolving bolts bored down into the bone.

The father ran the boat to O'Brien's camp in Wells Pass where there was a wireless telephone and the *Columbia* was contacted through Alert Bay. The call was just in time, as she was up Charles Creek and needed the full tide to get out; there would have been a 12-hour wait once the tide went down. The hospital ship got the child to Alert Bay Hospital and in three weeks the leg was completely healed. The grateful mother wrote: "This is only one typical instance of the invaluable services freely given by the Columbia Coast Mission to the isolated coast dwellers. Everywhere on the British Columbia coast are to be found hundreds of men and women and children, ourselves among them, who look forward to the visit of a dear friend. Always kind, and eager to help us..."

One woman, Alice Adams, expressed herself in a poem:

"May the mission ship *Columbia*
As it sails upon the sea,
Bring happiness to others
As it has brought to me."[5]

Due to the many trips that Antle was forced to make to England and eastern Canada to raise money for the establishment and upkeep of new ships and hospitals, a skipper, Ed Godfrey, was appointed to the *Columbia* in 1929 with a salary of $100 a month. Godfrey had been a lieutenant in the Royal Navy, serving in the Mediterranean and Adriatic, and before joining the mission had sailed in coastwise ships and qualified for his master's certificate. Cecil Fitzgerald, engineer, drew $110 as he also serviced the hospital lighting. Herschel Stringer (born on Herschel Island while his father was Archbishop of Rupert's Land) received $200 as doctor, and the very popular and versatile cook, Tony Katsumato, was paid $60. Good-natured Tony was with the mission for many

years and died in service; during his long tenure he had learned to substitute in emergencies for almost every job on board.
"... loved and mourned by all who knew him, Tony the in-
comparable. Shall we ever see his like again?" wrote Antle in
his Memoirs after Tony's death.

Chapter Three

To the Rescue
in Depression Days

I

A new little boat, the *Fredna*, was loaned to the fleet by Colonel Codville of Egmont in 1930. Built in 1912 by Menchions in Vancouver, she was 29 feet in length. She served the mission for a number of years, her skippers Canon Geoffrey D'Easum and the Reverend Sidney Holmes; with Pender Harbour as her home port she travelled south to Sechelt and Lasqueti and throughout the Jervis Inlet area up to Egmont. The small community of Egmont, surrounded by mountains on all sides, extended itself on each side of the inlet and on several little islands in between. Travel was by sea, as there were no roads and no cars, only woodland paths, so the forests were full of chattering squirrels and a variety of songbirds.

The *Fredna* was plagued with engine trouble. John Antle tried her out on a trip in the early summer of 1931, with Dr. Hill of the provincial government laboratories as guest and crew. After a few days of sailing up Jervis Inlet they were forced to return ignominiously to Pender Harbour at the end of a tow rope. In late September Antle tried her again with Herbert Spracklin as crew. They limped by slow stages to the Quathiaski machine shop and halted for repairs, then made it to Granite Bay and over to Rock Bay, but had to abandon the plan to visit Kingcome as so much time had been lost. Like a temperamental female, as soon as she reached Pender Harbour the *Fredna* speeded up and got them to Terranova Cannery on the arm of the Fraser in record time.

The *Fredna* had made an earlier successful trip to Hardy Island, bringing 80-year-old Mr. Paratt to the new St. Mary's Hospital in Pender Harbour, a five-mile journey. Along with the *Columbia* and the *Rendezvous*, she was in harbour for the opening of this little hospital on August 16, 1930. She was sold to James Dick of Cumberland in 1934, to Andrews and George of Vancouver in 1943 and to Bloedel Stewart and Welch Ltd. in 1945. An unlucky little ship, she sank in Great Central Lake on Vancouver Island in 1949, a total loss.

John Antle was convinced that the new district of Pender Harbour and Jervis Inlet must supply medical as well as spiritual service. In January 1930 he arranged for a little floating hospital that stood on a log raft at O'Brien Bay off Simoom Sound to be towed south by tug to Pender Harbour as it was no longer in use in the north. A fierce gale was encountered in Johnstone Strait and the floating hospital was wrecked. Before the sea was clear of wreckage, Antle was making plans for a larger structure built ashore. He started a subscription and canvassed widely once again, travelling to Victoria and Ottawa to gain support from provincial and federal governments. As a result the federal government built the road and retaining wall that led to the hospital. The site was donated by R. Brynildsen, Sr.

On August 16, 1930, the S.S. *Princess Patricia* arrived from Vancouver bearing spectators and the official party, including John Antle who recited a brief history of the Columbia Coast Mission's 25 years to that date. Archdeacon Heathcote gave the prayer of dedication and the formal opening of St. Mary's Hospital was performed by Lieutenant-Governor R. Randolph Bruce. At the opening, the hospital contained 12 beds, two solariums, a maternity room, nursery, caseroom and operating room. There were also x-ray and electrical-therapy departments. Staff at the opening were Dr. C. H. Ployart, Dr. I. B. Thompson, and nurse Bessie Newbolt assisted by Marion

Antle, John Antle's daughter. Mrs. Bradley was cook and George Bradley was orderly.

The marine mission was now in charge of three well-equipped hospitals, three ships and a staff of over 40. Unfortunately, expansion coincided with the Depression years. Funds were low. Patients in many cases paid their bills with vegetables or fruit in lieu of cash. Logging camps reflected the hard times prevalent up and down the coast. Many shut down. The Hastings Mill Company left the northern area, and though Merril, Ring and Wilson Logging Company took over for a few years, loggers were hard up for the most part and in Rock Bay few of them took out insurance, formerly a steady source of support for St. Michael's Hospital.

The mission was financed through various sources: a provincial grant; federal grants for Indian work; an annual grant from the British Columbia and Yukon Church Aid Society based in London; donations from the Missionary Society of the Church in Canada, based in Toronto, which responded to campaigns organized every two years by Antle; the dollar-a-month mission plan for medical service, and individual donations. Antle spoke to many church congregations across the country and collected considerable funds through his compelling eloquence; his success was viewed with mixed feelings by some of the incumbent pastors.

During the Depression, the Vancouver Welfare Federation gave large grants, but Vancouver citizens protested against assistance outside the city. Ernest Evans of the federation wrote a dramatic letter explaining the work and needs of the mission. Reproduced in *The Log*, it gives three examples of S.O.S. emergency calls received by the *Columbia*: a logging camp accident, a woman in premature labour in an isolated cabin up the coast and a sick child in one of the floating villages up a lonely inlet. During the previous year, emergency calls had involved 4,000 miles of travel in addition to the ship's regular 17,000 mile round; the doctor had received 636 patients on board and answered 547 calls to homes.

Answering the complaints of Vancouver citizens, he wrote: "The loggers, the fishermen, are Vancouver people, a lot of them, their families are here. They all buy here, send their money here; the logs they cut, the fish they catch, are processed and give employment here.

"What percentage of the settlers who need the ministrations of the Columbia Coast Mission from time to time, but who are making honest effort to support themselves and their families on the coast frontier would otherwise be on relief in Vancouver or a charge upon the local Welfare Federation?"

However, none of the grants were consistently forthcoming, and many were cut if the board disagreed with Antle's policies. The Columbia Coast Mission Board to whom Antle was responsible also clipped short many of Antle's expansive schemes. He envied the Grenfell Mission whose board concerned itself with raising money and did not interfere with mission projects.

Antle had many photographs and newsreels made of the activities of the *Columbia* to display to audiences during his appeals for funds. His newsreels recorded emergency cases brought out from the woods and treated on board or run to St. George's Hospital in Alert Bay. There were also scenes of christenings, confirmation classes and marriages. He had, however, no record on movie film of burials at sea which, as a sailor, he believed to be a particularly clean, sensible method. He could show his audiences how the mission served the people at birth, adolescence and maturity, but surely it was fitting to show that the cycle was completed as the ships committed to the deep certain of the parishioners whose lives had come to an end.

He was reluctant to film an actual burial at sea. Relatives might take offence if a ceremony deeply affecting to them were shown across the country to strangers as a means of encouraging viewers to subscribe to the mission. He discussed with Cecil Fitzgerald the possibility of filming a mock ceremony with a simulated body. Fitzgerald was to prepare the props, run the movie camera and assemble a group of mourners.

In burials at sea, the body is sewn into a canvas shroud which is heavily weighted at one end to carry the corpse quickly to the depths of the ocean. Fitzgerald stuffed the canvas sack in a realistic manner, though he had difficulty persuading the crew to part with much heavy iron piping, bolts, or other weights for a mock funeral. Eventually all was in readiness, a group of willing loggers was assembled on deck along with Antle and the crew, and Fitzgerald stood on top of the cabin with his movie apparatus set up.

All went well at first. Antle in his robes of office read the service, the canvas sack was hoisted to the railing and tipped up, the weights carried it over and into the ocean, and it sank beneath the surface.

After this, the procedure was to sail in a circle around the spot of burial, dropping wreaths into the sea at intervals. Then the ship would sound its whistle twice in farewell and depart, leaving the wreaths encircling the spot as they floated on the surface.

The ship made a half circle, dropping wreaths, and was heading back to the starting point when suddenly the canvas sack popped up. The weights kept the lower half under water but were insufficient to keep the upper section submerged. Bobbing gently in the waves, the mock corpse appeared to bow cheerfully to the startled mourners. Fitzgerald continued to crank his camera obediently until Antle shouted for him to cut. What happened to the film, Fitzgerald never knew, but he was relieved to see Antle give a grim smile as he prepared to head the *Columbia* away from the scene of the fiasco.

2

Despite financial problems, the ships kept to their schedules, performing innumerable services outside their regular line of duty; heartwarming services that did much to waken that affection with which so many citizens of British Columbia still remember the ships of the Columbia Coast Mission. Captain Godfrey of the *Columbia* sighted 15 sections of logs adrift off Port Hardy and turned aside to tow them to safety in a sheltered cove; the same month he towed Sam May's floating home from Simoom Sound to Tribune Channel, a distance of eight miles. The *Columbia* paused to aid seven Indians in a dugout canoe overloaded with supplies, towing them from Simoom Sound to Kingcome.

The *Rendezvous* delivered a kitten to Dr. Anderson at Alert Bay and a pet fawn to Percy Pike and his wife who ran the lighthouse at Pine Island. Messages and news were carried from one stop to another by obliging crews, and items of interest noted for inclusion in *The Log*, to be eagerly read by dwellers in remote areas. Some of these in the 1930s included:

"Thurston Bay: Bill Bachelor at Thurston Bay shoots cougar to get an appetite for breakfast in the morning. Awakened early one morning by one prowling around the house, he went out to investigate, clad only in his pyjamas. He found the cougar in his back yard and shot it."

"McKenzie Sound: Jim Dempsey is commencing logging operations again."

"Bones Bay: Jack Dorman and staff have arrived at the cannery."

"Rock Bay: Mr. J. Rankin Robertson of Whaletown spent some time in the hospital following a severe accident to his left foot."

"Grassey Bay: Mr. Geo. Byers has had the misfortune to lose all his goslings owing to the depredations of a large wolf."

"Blunden Harbour: Harry Darke has moved all his farm onto floats and is waiting for good weather to be towed into Wells Pass. Harry is one of the last of the original settlers in Blunden Harbour to leave."

A former resident of British Columbia wrote from Saskatoon, Saskatchewan: "Living, as we did, off the regular run of the Coast line freighters, the Mission ship 'Columbia', flagship of the fleet, well known in Vancouver waters, brought us our mail and food supplies over a period of months. When my young son was badly hurt, the 'Columbia' immediately responded to a call for help... It was but one instance of the practical help given to those who live in the isolated Coast areas north of Vancouver. The never failing courtesy, sympathy and generosity will always be a cherished memory. No one was forgotten at Christmas time..." [1]

Some families were watched over by the mission boats for years on end. The Strange sisters, Alice and Patty, and their brother Charlie were parishioners of John Antle in Vancouver before the formation of the mission. They were living on Camp Island when Antle called on them in the *Laverock* in 1904. Later they moved to Whaletown on Cortes where Charlie ran a little sawmill and Patty laboured all day to stoke the boiler and keep the steam up. They were struggling to make ends meet, but Alice produced every year the same decorative sheaf of wheat for the Harvest Festival at the Whaletown church and a plum pudding for each church party at Christmas.

After Charlie died, Patty's mind deteriorated. Perhaps due to her years of firing the boiler, she became terrified of fire, and no matter how cold the weather, would put out the kitchen stove as fast as Alice lit it. Then Alice fell and broke her hip and was taken in the *Rendezvous* to St. Mary's Hospital where she died in 1937. Poor Patty was the lone survivor of the three. Alan Greene made many visits to her, vainly trying to persuade her to leave her lonely cabin. She still distrusted fires, and with some embarrassment asked the chaplain to write to town to order some heavy underwear for her. The parcel arrived, and to her dismay was found to contain abbreviated garments of silk. The obliging chaplain composed another letter that blasted the shipper and quickly produced the warm longjohns needed to combat the cold in the little shack. Eventually he was able to take her in the *Rendezvous* to the hospital at Pender Harbour where she could be cared for by sympathetic nurses.

There were many burials at sea from the decks of the mission ships. One elderly parishioner left explicit instructions with Greene for his burial service: "Wrap me up in some clean white canvas, attach a boom chain to my heels, a red ensign around me, a short plank over the starboard quarter of the *Rendezvous*, you reading the committal service for those at sea, and Mr. Fitzgerald 'standing by' to launch me off, somewhere in the Gulf. Above all, I don't want anything to do with the cemetery . . . I prefer being in the Gulf in a south-easter— free. I rely upon you and Fitz, my good friends, to keep me

Official opening of St. Mary's Hospital, Pender Harbour, August 16, 1930. (*Courtesy Vancouver School of Theology*)

Mission boats *Columbia, Rendezvous* and *Fredna* (right to left) and C.P.'s *Princess Patricia* at opening of St. Mary's Hospital, Pender Harbour, August 16, 1930. (*Courtesy Vancouver School of Theology*)

Raising the mast on the *John Antle*, London, 1933. Rev. John Antle far right. (*Courtesy Vancouver School of Theology*)

Dedication of the first *John Antle* at Lambeth Pier, London, Bishop Winnington Ingram officiating, June 13, 1933. (*Courtesy Vancouver School of Theology*)

The first *John Antle*, 1933. (*Courtesy Vancouver School of Theology*)

Dr. Herschel Stringer, Capt. Ed Godfrey, Cecil Fitzgerald (engineer), crew of second *Columbia*, c. 1930. (*Courtesy Vancouver School of Theology*)

Figurehead of the *Syrene*, removed when she became the *John Antle*. Now at Royal Vancouver Yacht Club. (*Courtesy Ernest Antle*)

The first *Rendezvous* with C.H. Fitzgerald, c. 1930. (*Courtesy Vancouver School of Theology*)

Burial at sea from the second *Columbia*, c. 1934, Rev. B.H.L. Dance officiating. (*Courtesy C.G. Tuck*)

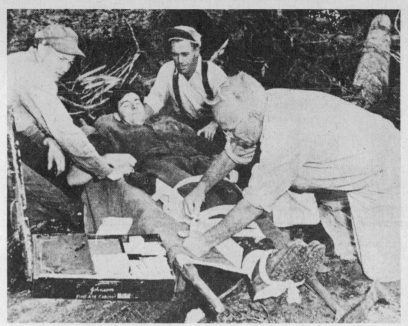

First aid in the woods, before moving patient aboard *Columbia*. (*From* The Log)

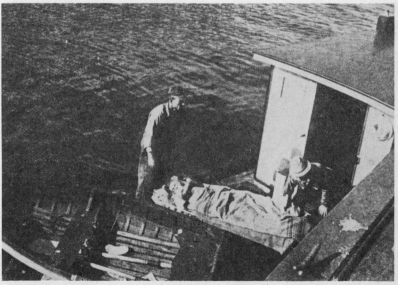

A badly injured logger is transferred to the second *Columbia*. (*From* The Log.)

Jack Morrill (cook), Dr. Connold, (skipper), Wally Smith (engineer) aboard second *John Antle,* 1936. (*Courtesy C.G. Tuck*)

Doug Morton, (skipper-engineer of *Rendezvous*) nurse Kay Krag and Dr. Keith Wray-Johnston at Rock Bay hospital, 1936. (*Courtesy Alan F. Greene*)

The *Florida V,* 1936, later the second *John Antle. (Courtesy C.G. Tuck)*

The first *Rendezvous* with picnic group at Okisollo Channel, 1937. Rev. Alan Greene second from left. (*Courtesy Doug Morton*)

A typical floathouse. (*Courtesy Dr. Keith Whittaker*)

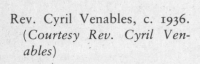

Rev. Cyril Venables, c. 1936. (*Courtesy Rev. Cyril Venables*)

Dr. G.E. Bayfield inoculating Indian children. (*Courtesy Mr. & Mrs. J.T. Bayfield*)

Capt. MacDonald, Dick French, "Auchie", Dr. Wace, Ted
Weddell, (deckhand) Mrs. MacDonald at window, on *Columbia*,
1939. (*Courtesy Mrs. G. MacDonald*)

Capt. and Mrs. MacDonald and *Columbia*'s doctor visit Mrs.
Harvey Mann at floating camp, Simoom Sound, 1939. (*Courtesy
Mrs. G. MacDonald*)

Capt. MacDonald, Dr. Gordon Worsley, Ben Drew, C.C.M. secretary, on *Columbia*, c. 1939.(*Courtesy Mrs. G. MacDonald*)

Rev. Alan Greene, Capt. MacDonald, Dick French, (engineer) Dr. Bayfield, Major Harding and "Auchie" (cook) in front, 1939. (*Courtesy Mrs. G. MacDonald*)

out of the cemetery." ² They followed his instructions, burying him at sea, under the lea of Harwood Island in the Gulf—free.

Despite the Depression, many young couples chose to face the difficulties together, and the mission boats played their part in the wedding ceremonies. John Antle performed a wedding service in 1930 for the daughter of Ernest Halliday, Ida Dorothy, who married John Errington on the *Columbia*. The wedding party came downriver in small boats, and after the ceremony the bride and groom took off in a launch in mist and rain, to honeymoon at Chop Bay. The following year the bride's sister Jean married Robert Duggan of Rock Bay, the wedding taking place in the Halliday home. This time when groom and attendants arrived, the tide was too low to get them ashore, so they spent the night on the *Rendezvous,* three ladies in the bunks and the men on the floor.

1931 also saw the wedding of the popular engineer Cecil Fitzgerald to Grace Anne Stothers of Buttres, Saskatchewan, the first couple to be married in St. Peter's Anglican Church in Campbell River. The bride was formerly a nurse at St. George's Hospital in Alert Bay, and the Fitzgeralds made their first home there in the *Columbia*'s home port. Captain Godfrey of the *Columbia* acted as best man for his handsome Irish engineer.

The Christmas cruises of the *Columbia, Rendezvous* and succeeding ships of the mission became a yearly event eagerly anticipated along the routes, and appointed dates were always kept by the ships except in the most violent storms. Accounts of two of the stops on Christmas cruises of the *Rendezvous* in the early 1930s show something of the heroic efforts of both entertainers and entertained to reach the scene of the concerts.

On December 10, laden with gifts for the many children on the route, the *Rendezvous* left Quathiaski Cove in a howling southeaster and pouring rain, bound for Owen Bay in the south of Sonora Island. By afternoon they reached the bay, and shortly afterwards two launches arrived from the Yaculta Rapids area, bringing a crowd aboard for the party. About 30 in all gathered in a little schoolhouse at the head of a slough for a programme that lasted until one in the morning.

The evening began with songs by the children, followed by a short service, then a skit entitled "Who Wouldn't be a Country Storekeeper?" and performed by Greene and Fitzgerald ("very laughable" wrote Greene). Movies were run with the hand-cranked machine, after which came the grand finale of the Christmas tree and distribution of presents. Throughout, the storm battered at the little building, tearing down a part of the chimney. Guests from the north were unable to leave until slack tide calmed the rapids, so the celebration continued with a dance in the Schiblers' float house.

A Christmas visit to Maurelle Island involved a concert in Miss Mrus's school, the one school on the island, in existence only five years as before and after that period the sparsely settled island was unable to produce enough children to meet the quota required by the government.

To get the invalid Mrs. Patterson to the concert, her daughters rounded up the one horse on the island, tucked their mother into a long flat sleigh filled with straw and drove her three miles to the beach. Next she was rowed through the rapids of Surge Narrows to Bill Heinbockel's shack, reaching shore by inching her way over a long slippery boom-stick, clinging to daughters fore and aft. (Heinbockel was an obliging bachelor who the year before had spent a whole day cooking in order to feed 40 persons at the Christmas concert, seating them in his little shack in relays of ten.) After a rest at Heinbockel's, Mrs. Patterson was helped along a woodland trail that involved the crossing of several small gorges by means of logs laid across them. At the close of the concert, Heinbockel put her up for the night in his cabin, and the next morning the *Rendezvous* carried her to the cove where horse and sleigh waited near the beach. Cecil Fitzgerald rowed Mrs. Patterson ashore and delivered her, exhausted but exhilarated, to the care of her daughters.

3

An important part of the *Columbia*'s work involved the northern Kwakiutl Indian villages at Alert Bay and Kingcome. The *Columbia* called in frequently at Kingcome, for Ernest

Halliday, brother of the Indian Agent, was always ready with a warm welcome at any hour of the day or night. He and his wife had settled at the head of Kingcome Inlet in 1894. Medical care, baptisms and weddings were available for Indians whom Halliday brought to the attention of the *Columbia*, but in the 1920s ten Indian chiefs wrote to Antle asking for an Indian school and church services, which Antle was anxious to provide. If the board hesitated, Antle declared, "the Methodists are ready and willing to step in with both..."

After 1927, Kingcome and the adjacent island villages, formerly under the administration of the two dioceses, were serviced by the Columbia Coast Mission. Antle obtained funds of an English missionary society, the New England Company, formed in Kent in the days of Cromwell. The company had been instituted by an Act of the Long Parliament in 1649 to propagate "the Gospel of Jesus Christ in New England." When the United States ceased to be an English colony, the funds were diverted to the Church in Canada, particularly for work among the Indians. They had been held in trust by the Bishop of New Westminster for half a century. Kingcome, on the mainland, was in the bishop's New Westminster diocese. With this money, and with assistance from the Indian Affairs Branch, Antle built a large mission house at Kingcome with a day school, dispensary and living quarters for the missionary, all under one roof.

Now the villages were placed on the *Columbia*'s regular run. She was eagerly awaited at Village Island where two women missionaries, Miss Kathleen O'Brien and her helper Miss Nixon toiled alone as nurse, missionaries and teachers. The *Columbia* had towed their float house to the island, and their little school was built at Miss O'Brien's own expense with the help of the Reverend Comley, then of Alert Bay. A small preventorium to care for T.B. patients, which the Indians called "*Huyatsi*," meaning a place of healing, was also paid for by Miss O'Brien, who received the M.B.E. in 1940 for her work. Antle believed the small schools on these reserves engendered better relations with the Indians than did the large boarding schools where children were separated from their parents.

The method of payment by the Indians for medical expenses at Alert Bay was settled by having the Indians pay a fixed sum each year after the fishing season. As always, Antle was primarily interested in providing medical aid, remembering Dr. Hutton's quotation: "Heal the sick . . . and say unto them, the Kingdom of God is come nigh unto you." In 1919 Dr. Wilson had reported to him that 90% of the Indians of Alert Bay and adjacent islands were suffering from anaemia, scrofula, rheumatism, enlarged tonsils and adenoids, deafness, blindness and venereal disease. Seventy percent were victims of tuberculosis.

Antle also sympathized with the Indians in their fight to regain the right to hold their potlatches, a fight not won until 1951. He believed that whisky pedlars who supplied the potlatches with drink were the main problem. Antle and Greene travelled on the *Columbia* in 1931 to inspect the northern area. At Kingcome, Chief Johnny Scow of Kingcome told them potlatches were the backbone of the Indians' social life, and the Potlatch Law of 1884 had left them "without joy or pleasure." A report which followed in *The Log* stated: "When all is said and done, the Indian has borne with a great deal of patience an outrageous attack upon his liberty scarcely equalled in the annals of British colonization . . . I am on the side of the Indian." In this Antle differed from many of the missionaries on the coast who were virulent in their attacks on the potlatch ceremonies and dances.

4

More than once the *Rendezvous* ran on the rocks as she cruised the coast during all seasons of the year. One bitterly cold New Year's Day Alan Greene was travelling south, and about 15 miles north of Rock Bay discovered that the ship's water tank was nearly empty. Whenever they came to a wharf with a water system laid down they found the water frozen solid. Then as they passed near shore they noticed a cascade of water plunging down the side of a cliff and into the sea. A splendid solution suggested itself: the *Rendezvous* would run in close until her nose was under the cascade, which they would direct into the water tank.

All went well until they cast off, whereupon the engine spluttered to a stop, and before they could start it up the strong tide swept the ship hard aground on a bare rock that lay directly in their course. The tide was falling, and the crew leapt out on the rock, trying first to shove the ship free, and when this failed, rowing ashore to collect small logs to force in under the hull. These would form a skidway down which the *Rendezvous* could slide if she dislodged herself when the tide went down.

The crew huddled in blankets on the bare rock as darkness descended, getting up at intervals throughout the night to see if their shoring was holding her steady. A vessel passed once, creating waves that might easily have tipped her over, but she stayed firm, clinging to the steep side of the rock until noon the next day when a high tide lifted her free. Fortunately, she had suffered no injury and was able to continue south to Rock Bay.

They were less fortunate one day in May when they ran on a rock not shown on their chart, at the south end of the Ragged Islands. These islands, now called the Copeland Islands, lie to the west of Malaspina Peninsula, not far from Desolation Sound. The *Rendezvous* was backed off on her own power when the tide rose, but was forced to limp to Vancouver Shipyards with a partially split stem and a shattered keel forward. She was repaired in time to make a trip with the body of Mrs. August Schnarr, wife of the well-known logger and cougar hunter, to Cameleon Harbour where Greene conducted the funeral service.

There were many pleasant periods interspersed among the storms and shipwrecks. Greene enjoyed them all, fine days and foul, cruising the coast and revelling in the freedom of the seas. By the white sands of Savary Island he wrote, ". . . the sea with its persistent yet restful wash on the beach, was nature's accompaniment to our act of worship."[3]

Doug Morton served on the *Rendezvous* for a number of

years during the 1930s, first as engineer for Alan Greene and then as skipper and engineer for the Reverend Cyril Venables. His recollections of those days give a picture of the work of the mission ships and the life of settlers and loggers. As Alan Greene's engineer he worked during the winter months, so his memories of those days are mainly of stormy sessions at sea. "We had calm, sunny days too," he says, "but one tends to remember the bad ones that put a scare in us."

On one occasion, the *Rendezvous* had engine trouble and the *Columbia* was towing her through the Hole-in-the-Wall Rapids on a rope that was tied around her cabin. When they hit the tide rip, the boats were carried in opposite directions; the rope shifted and effectively blocked the wheelhouse door. The *Rendezvous* heeled over, almost capsizing, far enough to fill the dinghy on top of the cabin with water. Greene scrambled through the little window over the steering wheel, certain the vessel was turning bottom up as she hit the shore with a wallop, but she righted herself as the *Columbia* threw off the towline and let her drift downstream before picking her up again.

The engine failed at the most ill-chosen moments. Coming around Cape Mudge in rough weather it sputtered to a stop and the waves carried them towards the beach as Greene struggled to get it going again. They were almost ashore when Morton saw the loose condenser that caused the trouble and tightened it up in time to keep the *Rendezvous* from smashing on the beach.

A near catastrophe of another kind occurred in calm weather. The *Rendezvous* set out from Manson's Landing, collecting patients at various points all the way to Owen Bay and conveying them, about 12 in all, to the hospital at Rock Bay for checkups. While the patients were ashore, Morton noticed that magazines stacked under the cabin steps were wet. Investigating, he found the wetness was gasoline. The fuel tank had sprung a leak and two inches of gas lay in the bilge, the full length of the boat. Several of the passengers had been smoking during the journey, and the thought of what might have happened made Morton's flesh creep. The gas was pumped out of the bilge and it was well scrubbed, but NO

SMOKING was the order given on the return trip.

The beauty of the fiords in the north and the smooth sandy beaches on many of the islands gladdened the hearts of the crews on warm, sunny days. Desolation Sound, so depressing to Captain Vancouver, is one of the world's beauty spots in fine weather, its waters smooth and blue, its green islands surrounded by snow-topped mountains. In such weather, Alan Greene gathered up settlers in the *Rendezvous* and took them for picnics in some pleasant spot.

Chaplain Greene was always given a welcome by settlers and loggers, according to Doug Morton. He was unfailingly cheerful and generous with time and service. Morton remembers that Greene loaned him the *Rendezvous* after Doug married Jenny Hunt of Quathiaski, and the newlyweds sailed over to Gorge Harbour for their honeymoon.

5

John Antle had been canvassing for funds in England once more, to add a new ship to his fleet. In 1933 the B.C. and Yukon Church Aid Society, a missionary society based in England, donated funds for the purchase of the *Syrene*, a private yacht owned originally by a Greek millionaire, who had the instrument panel labelled in Greek letters. Antle acquired her in Cannes, and sailed her to Gibraltar where he had two new engines installed to replace the originals which had broken down *en route*.

The trip from Cannes involved a comedy of errors. Antle had taken on two young Canadians as crew and a Frenchman as engineer. A storm blew up and Antle decided to seek a sheltered port. As the ship bucked the waves, the two Canadian boys were seasick, the lighting equipment failed, and Antle, struggling to remember schoolboy French, tried to direct his French engineer and to decipher the Greek lettering on the instrument panel with the aid of a flashlight.

From Gibraltar the *Syrene* was taken to London for the dedication service. Bishop Winnington Ingram dedicated the ship at Lambeth Pier on June 13, 1933, giving her a new name, the *John Antle*. She would replace the tiny *Fredna* on the Jervis Inlet and Lasqueti Island run, with headquarters at Pender Harbour, and John Antle would be her skipper.

Antle planned to sail her home from England via the Panama Canal, a trip of nearly 11,000 miles. It was a voyage that caught the imagination of the public, and newspapers reported every stage of the long journey. Antle's crew consisted of Lieutenant R.V.A. Corbett, R.N.R., who acted as navigator and mate; R. Phillips, a former Malaya planter who served as quartermaster; E.W. Soutar, engineer; H. Connor, cook, and Oscar Nurse who joined the vessel at San Pedro. A voluntary crew included a son of the Honourable F.D. Burden, and P.H. Keeling, son of the Reverend W.T. Keeling of Vancouver.

The log of the four-month voyage reads as follows:

	Miles
July 31 — left London	
Aug. 2 — ar. Falmouth	322
Aug. 4 — left Falmouth	
Aug. 11 — ar. Las Palmas	1428
Aug. 17 — left Las Palmas	
Aug. 21 — ar. St. Vincent, Cape Verde Is	874
Aug. 22 — left Cape Verde Islands	
Sept. 5 — ar. Port of Spain, Trinidad	2441
Sept. 8 — left Port of Spain	
Sept. 10 — ar. Curacao	477
Sept. 12 — left Curacao	
Sept. 16 — ar. Colon	707
Sept. 18 — transit of Canal, Colon to Balboa	43
Oct. 5 — left Balboa	
Oct. 22 — ar. San Pedro	2999
Nov. 7 — left San Pedro	
Nov. 13 — ar. William Head	1094
Nov. 14 — ar. Victoria, B.C.	10
Nov. 20 — ar. Vancouver, B.C.	83
Total mileage	10,478

There had been fine weather all the way, until they arrived in Victoria and were met by a dense fog. During the 2441 miles between St. Vincent and Trinidad the ship had developed some engine defects which slowed her, and she had run out of water and fuel before she made port. This, however, had been her only trouble during the long voyage.

Her beautiful mermaid figurehead, removed as unsuitable for a missionary ship, was given to the Royal Vancouver Yacht Club, where she still leans out from the club's balcony, gazing wistfully over the waters of English Bay.

The *John Antle* was a handsome ship with fine lines, 74 feet long, with a narrow beam. She had been built in 1921 at Hampton-on-Thames by Thornycrofts, with an inside finish of birds-eye maple and mahogany, double teak planking and copper rivets and bottom. Most of her accommodation was below deck but her deck-house was converted to a dispensary and first-aid hospital. Her first stint on the Pender Harbour route, starting September 17, 1934, was a short one, as after her Christmas run the funds for her upkeep were exhausted and she was tied up until the spring.

On Jubilee Day, May 6, she sailed for Lasqueti Island with flags fluttering at the mast heads and astern, in answer to an invitation to a barbecue and carnival to be held there. Antle had accepted with alacrity, seeing an excellent opportunity to advertise the medical services of the mission. He brought along the doctor from St. Mary's Hospital at Pender Harbour.

They anchored in beautiful, sheltered Scottie Cove, and as soon as they had rowed ashore to the smooth, sandy beach they were met by a worried mother with a small boy who had fallen and injured an arm and now had developed a lump in his neck. The doctor found the trouble to be a malunited fracture of the collar bone. The crew walked to False Bay where Mr. and Mrs. Williams, the storekeepers, revived them with tea and drove them to Tucker Bay, the scene of the barbecue. Mr. Norrish volunteered to drive the doctor to see a sick woman while the sheep were being roasted on spits before a huge log fire. After a long ride, they came to a house by the seashore where the patient was bedridden. Another bedridden patient was 12 miles away, with no road to her house, but she sent a young girl to describe her symptoms and ask for medicine.

Back at the barbecue the doctor found the master of ceremonies carving mutton and handing out sandwiches and coffee, but his share grew cold as a steady stream of patients sought his advice, retreating with him behind a blackboard set up to ensure privacy. In all, some 30 patients were seen and examined that day, and a long list of prescriptions was made, to be filled at the hospital. While this went on, Antle seized the opportunity to put forth a proposal whereby the residents could have hospital and medical attention by paying in kind; that is, by giving farm produce and fresh meat instead of money. He also told them that he had secured an order for 300 pounds of clipped wool for them. In those Depression years, the news was more than welcome to the Lasqueti farmers and sheep ranchers.

Meanwhile, the *Columbia* and *Rendezvous* continued their coverage of the northern and central areas. An emergency relief fund was formed on the *Columbia* with Dr. Gordon Kirkpatrick as the treasurer, to aid victims of the Depression in need of immediate relief while they waited for government help. There was no set programme of government relief at the time: sometimes there was a cash payment; groceries might be supplied; men might be sent to work on the roads or in relief camps; and fishermen received five dollars a month for food. The Columbia Coast Mission boats reached many isolated homes unvisited by social workers, and the missionaries felt their familiarity with the actual needs of the unemployed in their area resulted in a fairer distribution of aid. Provincial police and, later, government relief officers, made decisions which the mission sometimes considered unjust where funds were withheld due to lack of on-the-spot knowledge.

Throughout the Depression years, the superintendent's annual report speaks of clothing, bedding, and babies' layettes distributed by the boats. In 1938 the report to the board stated that cash received for social service work "made it possible to provide in some cases second-hand kitchen ranges . . . to replace worn-out kitchen ranges in some homes where difficult times made the purchase of a new stove impossible." Emergency requests were answered for "dentures, eye-glasses, school text-books, special advances to families where perhaps a mother must go to Vancouver to consult a specialist, advances to a fisherman for a herring-net, the purchase of milking goats where a little homestead in its early stages lacks the funds and pasturage for a cow..." Eagerly received as well was the "literature by the ton" handed out from the ships' libraries to homes and camps in remote areas.

The *Columbia* covered an average of 90 ports of call on each of her rounds in the 1930s. On her Christmas tour of camps and settlements in 1934 she made 27 stops, with Fitzgerald playing Santa, running the projector and distributing toys, candies and fruit to the children. The ship kept in touch with Alert Bay during the tours, and movies ended abruptly if an emergency call came through.

During the life of the Columbia Coast Mission marine service there was always a tremendous turnover of staff. Pay was necessarily small in comparison with shore work in the cities. Doctors, ship crews and clergy came and went at an alarming rate, with many temporary substitutes filling in until others were found who would sign on for what was hoped would be a longer period. Few possessed the undying enthusiasm that inspired John Antle and Alan Greene. Only those with a deep love of the sea, of solitude, and of the communion with nature and their own thoughts and beliefs afforded by the long trips up the rugged coast, were satisfied to stay many years with the marine mission.

Low pay, southeaster storms, treks through the bush, and the absence of the city's creature comforts took their toll. Some clergymen missed the gracious services in the large churches filled with sympathetic believers. Setting up a portable altar on a lonely beach or contending with the many aggressive arguments was apt to rob them of their missionary zeal. Some would have stayed longer but were called by the bishop to fill posts in parish churches, positions always deemed of primary importance by the prelates.

There were also those who disagreed with Antle's emphasis on medical and social aid, sometimes resulting in the minimizing of the spiritual work. The Reverend B.H.L. Dance who had worked with Greene for a winter on the *Rendezvous* and succeeded the Reverend Thompson on the *Columbia* in 1933, disagreed with Antle's priorities. He said he "was unable to carry out adequately his religious duties"[4] and feared the reduction of the *Columbia* to a purely itinerant hospital ship. He left the mission in 1936 to take charge of the church in Alert Bay.

Yet many who served for short periods retain vivid and happy memories of their days with the mission. Dr. Keith Whittaker took charge of St. Michael's Hospital at Rock Bay in 1935, succeeding Dr. Gordon Kirkpatrick, and also served for a short time at St. George's Hospital in Alert Bay and on the *Columbia*. Now an octogenarian living in Ontario, he tells of the lonely settlers who welcomed the *Columbia* and the news she bore of distant friends and neighbours. He remembers calling at logging camps and marvelling at the enormous meals that provided the energy required by loggers for their demanding work: a groaning board that included three or four kinds of hot meat, vast amounts of potatoes and vegetables and several varieties of pies. He recalls the beautiful coastal scenery of mountains and sea, and the need for an expert knowledge of navigation when the ship was forced to buck the tide in the treacherous narrows to answer an emergency call. In those days, he says, it was essential that a medical man on the upper coast be "capable of doing anything that might come his way."[5]

6

In 1936 John Antle, the old warrior, retired from the mission at the age of 70. At this time there were three hospitals, five churches, two Indian missions (at Kingcome and Village Island), the hospital ship *Columbia* and two missionary or ambulance ships in service. He could look back on a battle

86

well fought, with the results of his victories openly in evidence. He once said to his assistant: "Greene, I think there's something wrong with the man who has made no enemies."[6] He may have ruffled the feathers of some who resented his fierce drive towards his objective and his outspoken criticism of ineptitude that might delay attainment of his goal, but he won their respect. He was demanding of others, but he was still more demanding of himself. Many hundreds would remember the courage and determination that took him through the fiercest storms in answer to a call of distress.

A writer[7] has said that Antle was one of those rare individuals who combine vision and practicality; who possess the ability to carry their visions to a practical conclusion. Robson Black in *The American Magazine* wrote: "The Dominion of Canada is bounded on the east by Wilfred Grenfell and on the west by John Antle."[8] Words that might be applied to him are those of the apostle Peter: "He went about doing good."

Antle retired with few of the honours that his work deserved, beyond a Doctor of Divinity degree in 1937 conferred by St. John's College, Winnipeg, on the recommendation of the Bishop of Columbia. The Reverend J.W. Matheson, M.A., D.D., in his address at the ceremony, said in part: "There are two men who have been doing a great work in Canada during the past 30 odd years, a work so unique as to render comparison with any other philanthropic effort out of place, and yet so similar as to justify the collocation of their names. They are Dr. Grenfell and the Rev. John Antle.

"Because it was the only way to reach those whom they wished to serve, they both (to use the Psalmist's words) 'went down to the sea in ships and occupied their business in great waters.' They both brought medical skill, hospitals, nurses, schools, and all the blessings and privileges of the Evangel in their ships,—Dr. Grenfell to the isolated groups of fisher folks along the rugged shores of Labrador—Mr. Antle to the scattered groups of lumber jacks, fishermen and Indians along the northwest coast of British Columbia.

"...What labours, what planning, what disappointments, what opposition he had to encounter during those 30 years.... Suffice it to say that the Columbia Coast Mission is a going concern, acknowledged on all sides as a great achievement..."

Retirement to Antle meant time to answer the call of adventure, the call of the sea that never ceased its siren song for him, from childhood until his death. In 1939 he went to England to collect a 40–foot yacht, the *Reverie,* that he had purchased sight unseen in exchange for his property at Maple Bay. Long a widower, he said, "My boat is my home, and I can live anywhere I like."

The *Reverie* had been built about 1934 in Assam, India, and had been taken 800 miles by rail to the coast and then by freighter to England, where she was launched in the Thames. Antle sailed in her from Falmouth on August 11, 1939, and reached Victoria, British Columbia, 13 months later, going by way of the Panama Canal. On August 25 he reached Lisbon, and arrived at Funchal, Madeira, on September 7. Off Funchal two German submarines were sighted, but he continued on his course. "I figured the U-boats wouldn't waste a torpedo on a yawl," he said nonchalantly.[9]

He stayed in Madeira for two months, tutoring two English boys aboard his ship, to augment his slender funds. His amateur crew left him there, except for a Portuguese lad who could speak no English. Antle repaid the boy for his fidelity when they got back to Vancouver by persuading immigration authorities to grant his wish to remain in the country. They cruised the Virgin Islands in January and reached the Panama Canal March 31. From Panama to Acapulco the *Reverie* encountered terrible storms, "next door to hurricane" that swept her decks and tossed the ship like a cork.[10] Her sails were ripped to shreds. By the time Antle found shelter along the Mexican coast he had run out of food, and after he paid the exorbitant Customs fees at Acapulco he had only two shillings left. Mexican fishermen grubstaked him and someone gave him a set of sails to continue his journey.

The *Reverie* rolled considerably because of her narrow

beam, but Antle kept her far off-shore to pick up favourable winds. His family and friends at home had no word from him for 61 days, and great was the relief when he sailed into Victoria on September 17, 1940, bronzed and bearded, having celebrated his 75th birthday at sea. The Reverend Cyril Venables paddled out to the yacht in a canoe, climbed aboard and discovered Antle alone in the cabin.

"Good God, where did you come from?" said the startled voyager.

"I came out to greet you," Venables replied, taken aback by the gruff exclamation and by the captain's long beard cascading to his waist.

"Well, can you get me to a barber? I want to get rid of this," Antle said, patting the beard that rivalled that of the Ancient Mariner.

Venables was surprised to find that Antle was as nervous in an automobile as he was daring at sea. Driving through the streets in a heavy fog with Venables, he grew increasingly restless until eventually he asked to be let out and walked beside the car until they reached their destination. But on his ship, fog and storm held no terrors for him. "Despite all the hardships," he said, "I would make such a voyage again if I wasn't so old. At sea one forgets the troubles and cares of a war-torn world."[11]

The shortage of priests during the war moved Antle to return to parish work on Mayne Island, but once peace was declared he was eager to set sail again. Crewed by two young girls, Lucy Varty and Audrey Sherlock, the *Reverie* headed for the West Indies, with Antle hoping to continue on to New York and then to Newfoundland. He was 81. Illness and bad weather forced him to cancel the trip in San Francisco, and he returned home, leaving the *Reverie* to be sailed back by members of the Royal Vancouver Yacht Club. He lived on his beloved yacht, moored at the yacht club, until he suffered a stroke at 84.

From the boat he sent a message to Alan Greene to come to his aid, and Greene and Ernest Antle persuaded him, much against his will, to leave the *Reverie*. As he was helped to dress and was assisted from the boat he quoted gloomily, "'When thou wast young thou girdest thyself and walkedst whither thou wouldest, but when thou shalt be old thou shalt stretch forth thy hands, and another shall gird thee, and carry thee whither thou wouldest not.'"

With a momentary flash of his old raillery he added, "Do you know where that's from, Greene?"

Greene knew. "Yes, skipper, from the last chapter of the Gospel According to St. John."

For Antle, Greene would always be the boy from an inland town, untrained in deep sea navigation. "Good for you, Greene," he said kindly. "I didn't think you knew your Bible that well. You Wycliffe men are rather weak on the scriptures."

As they rode away in Ernest Antle's car, he began to reminisce about his boyhood days when he sailed his little skiff in the rough waters off the Newfoundland coast. He died at the home of his son Ernest a week later, on December 3, 1949. Present at the Requiem Mass held the day before the funeral was 90-year-old Father Lawrence Amor who had been pastor of the parish in Greenspond when Antle was sent there in 1890.

Antle was buried at sea from aboard the *Columbia*, with Canon Alan Greene reading the committal service. An escort of boats followed the mission ship out of the harbour, including power boats from the Royal Vancouver Yacht Club that Antle had helped to organize. The old ship's bell from the *Empress of Japan* had been brought on board, and eight bells were struck as the body slid into the water, half way between Passage and Bowen Islands in an area called Manson's Deep.

It was fitting that as the *Columbia* was heading towards this spot, the old *Syrene I* passed them, entering the harbour. She was the ship that John Antle had sailed out from England on his adventurous voyage in 1933, the first ship to bear his name. Under her new owner, the Minister of Lands in Victoria, she was once again the *Syrene I*. Seeing the *Columbia* with flag at half mast, the *Syrene* dipped her own ensign in tribute to the intrepid captain of the marine mission fleet.

Chapter Four

New Priorities:
The War Years

Alan Greene had become superintendent in 1936 when Antle retired. The two were unlike in every respect except for devotion to the mission and to the sea. Where Antle was slim, dark, reserved, his expression confident and commanding, Greene was short, plump, fair, and friendly as a puppy, with a penchant for puns and horseplay. With 20 years of experience with the mission, he was the obvious choice, but from this date the character and objectives of the mission gradually altered until the marine service was finally dissolved. Many factors contributed to the change, including the desire of the board's chairman, Bishop Sexton, to see the mission work become solely spiritual. Greene still hoped at this stage to retain Antle's original structure, emphasizing the medical end and fulfilling Antle's oft-repeated maxim: "The church should render service as well as hold services."[1] In his first report he listed each hospital with its attendant ship: St. Mary's with the *John Antle*, St. Michael's with the *Rendezvous*, and St. George's with the *Columbia*. The change came gradually, with the *Columbia* and her sister ships continuing the medical service and several new boats added to the fleet, but the trend now was towards spiritual and social rather than medical work.

In the year before his retirement, Antle had made three complete and two partial tours of his district with the first *John Antle,* but the Winthrop diesel engines that he had installed in Gibraltar proved unsuitable for northern waters and needed frequent costly repairs. Finally the ship was operating on only one engine, with insufficient power to carry her through winter storms. The B.C. and Yukon Church Aid Society (which had provided the boat and helped in its upkeep) was still fretting over the cost of the diesel engines that Antle had substituted (twice the cost of the boat) and had reduced its grant, with admonitions to Greene to emphasize the spiritual side of the work.

The cost of new engine replacement and other necessary alterations for the *John Antle* would approximate that of an alternative plan which Greene in his new capacity as superintendent laid before the board in the fall. This was the purchase of a converted seine-boat, the *Florida V*, from B.C. Packers. Built in 1924, she was 55 feet overall, with a diesel engine close to the requirements of a mission ship. The sale of the first *John Antle* would help defray the cost, with a $1500 mortgage owing to B.C. Packers. The board was agreeable, the first *John Antle* was sold to Harry R. Rendell of Vancouver who registered her under her original name, *Syrene I*, and the *Florida V* became the newest member of the fleet, her name altered to *John Antle*.

While the boat was still registered as *Florida V,* Alan Greene took a party on board for a trial run. They left Pender Harbour at ten in the morning, headed for Ballenas Island Lighthouse across the gulf. Greene was delighted to find a brisk southeaster blowing in the gulf, a good test for the new vessel, though his guests, including Canon Martin of Winnipeg, were less enthusiastic. They reached the Ballenas Islands around one and tied up to the log boom of two little tugs that had hove to in the shelter of the islands. At midnight, however, the wind dropped and the tow-boat men came alongside to say they were pulling out with their booms.

"All hands on deck!" was the order on the *Florida V,* and a motley crew, in pyjamas and odd bits of clothing hastily donned, helped to cast loose and get the ship to a new anchorage in Maggie Bay between the islands. "All part of life on the ocean wave," Greene told his guests, always impishly gleeful when dignitaries from the cities were given a taste of the dangers and discomforts of marine mission work.

In the morning the lighthouse keeper, Douglas Dane, and his wife came out in their boat for the first service held on the ship. Mr. Dane had been a relief engineer on the *Columbia* and his wife Bessie was a nurse in the mission hospitals before her marriage. The crew joined the guests in the cabin on the main deck, soon to become the chapel and hospital room, and after a simple communion service they closed with the appropriate hymn: "Jesus calls us o'er the tumult of our life's tempestuous sea."

Shortly after this, Mr. Dane had occasion to thank Greene for the prompt assistance of Dr. Connold and the *Florida V* when a guest at the lighthouse was taken very ill. Dane used his amateur radio station to contact another amateur radio station at Savary Island, which sent the message by land line to Pender Harbour. This was at five p.m., the ship left at 5:15, arrived at 8:15 and by 10:15 was on her way to the Pender Harbour hospital with the patient. "Here on this little island, so isolated," wrote Dane, "it is indeed very comforting to know that a doctor is within call and that he will come if humanly possible."[2]

Greene appointed the Reverend T.A. Lane Connold, M.D. as skipper, parson and doctor for the second *John Antle*, Wally Smith as engineer and Jack Morrill as cook-deckhand. Dr. Connold had joined the mission in 1934, taking charge of St. Mary's Hospital in Pender Harbour. Connold in his triple capacity ran the ship for a year on a regular route to Jervis and Sechelt Inlets, Halfmoon Bay, and to the lighthouses at Ballenas Island and Sister's Rock, after which he left the mission and returned to England.

Alan Greene's amiable nature and sociable disposition gained him considerable popularity among the settlers and a good many of the loggers. He and his wife were well-loved on Quadra Island, their home for many years, and the chaplain was in demand for weddings, baptisms and funerals up and down the coast. The Mansons allowed Greene to build a wooden platform on their property near the beach at Manson's Landing on Cortes Island. On this, Greene erected an enormous tent, large enough to accommodate himself and his wife and their five children. Many summer vacations were spent there by the chaplain and his family.

Greene also took his wife and children for holiday trips on the boats, as did most of the missionaries with families. There were stops for services even during vacations, Gertrude Greene enlivening them with solos sung in her lovely voice to the accompaniment of the portable organ. Her presence was a welcome interlude for Greene, as his wife provided the sort of meals seldom created by his cook-deckhands. Unfortunately, Gertrude was a poor sailor, unlike her husband, and a stiff summer westerly that rocked the boat would soon have her feeling queasy. There were usually other guests crowding the boat on the holiday cruises, often drawn to the galley to watch the cook in action. On one rough trip, she was experiencing the first waves of nausea as she cooked on an oil stove whose fumes filled the small cabin. A guest smoking a large cigar was moved to stand close beside her and watch every step of the preparations. This proved her final downfall. She got dinner on the table, then retreated to her bunk to suffer in solitude as guests and family enjoyed the fruits of her labour.

At the Christmas concerts in island schoolhouses, Greene entered into the spirit of the celebrations with gusto, shedding dignity without a qualm. His humour tended towards the slapstick, and he enjoyed simple puns, perpetrating a few in his columns in *The Log*. A prime showman, he made a practice of slowing down the action with his hand-cranked movie machine during exciting moments, to add to the suspense. He originated the peculiar custom with his Santa impersonations in which the suit was stuffed with inflated balloons. He would grab the children in a bear hug and the balloons would pop loudly, to the delight of small boys, though some more romantic youngsters were alarmed to see the saint lose his corpulence so swiftly and noisily. Elderly ladies were hugged tight and the red lipstick colouring Santa's nose was transferred to their own noses, causing more hilarity.

Greene's horseplay and comic performances seem to have been popular with young and old. Pioneer Mrs. Elmer Ellingsen of Hague Lake, Cortes Island, says: "One of our warmest memories of him is his annual impersonation of Santa Claus at the Christmas parties. He put a personal touch and humour into it and made it something everyone looked forward to. He came to our logging camp in Loughborough Inlet in 1939 to marry a couple who were working for us and stayed for the party that followed that evening. He always contributed much to the gathering."[3]

Greene took pride in lasting out the night at the settlers' lengthy, energetic dances that usually concluded the weddings at which he officiated. He shared their mirth while attempting a schottische, "gyrating like a flapping scarecrow", and tripped a light fantastic, he said, that was fantastic but never light.[4] Captains of tugboats, ferries and pleasure boats came to know the chaplain whose boat often berthed near their own in anchorages up and down the coast, and today they recollect his anecdotes with affection and amusement.

Mrs. Ellingsen writes of the time in the 1930s before her marriage when she lived on Hernando Island with her relatives, the Mansons, who owned property there as well as on Cortes. During the winters most of the Mansons went to Vancouver and May Ellingsen's father, her uncle Wilf Manson and her brother and herself were the only persons living on the whole island. She says: "Alan Greene called in to see us on occasion and brought us magazines and news from around the area. This was much appreciated and always a pleasant break in the regular routine. Alan Greene was always ready to lend a helping hand...I think the Columbia Coast Mission contributed in a very positive way to the everyday existence of families along the coast."[5]

The new superintendent appeared to have a genuine affection and sympathy for the settlers he contacted, and no task was beneath his dignity to perform if it brought aid and comfort to them. On the other hand, he enjoyed the celebrities—

royalty, governors-general, bishops and archdeacons—who were guests on his ships, and he relished these tastes of the clerical life he had known in Toronto. He was a highly successful publicity man, with many ideas for advertising the work of the mission. In his first year as superintendent, he gave 81 addresses in the east, at which close to 22,000 people were told of the work and needs of his organization. He always included human interest anecdotes, humorous and tragic, which were highly popular with listeners. He talked on CBC radio and took several short movies of the mission activities which were shown by the National Film Board in 1953. This was important, as the Anglican Church had none of the excellent financial organization of the United Church and depended on irregular contributions for its work.

2

In 1936 Greene went east on one of his publicity campaigns. A new chaplain, the Reverend Cyril Venables, took over from 1936 to 1938. His headquarters were at Quathiaski Cove, and his area covered the central portion of the mission territory with additional mileage from Rock Bay to Kelsey Bay and including the Salmon River valley, the whole adding up to 2000 square miles. In *The Log,* the superintendent urged the parishioners to await the new chaplain's visits with patience as he must first familiarize himself with the wild rapids of Seymour, the Yacultas, the Greene Point and Arran Rapids, Hole-in-the-Wall, Okisollo and Surge Narrows. It sounded an intimidating prospect for a novice, added to the job of finding his way through the bush to isolated homes and logging camps.

Doug Morton became skipper and engineer for Venables, a year-round job as the new chaplain had little experience with boats or rapids. The handsome young clergyman came to the marine mission afire with ambition to serve in a field where he believed the need was great. He was born in Enderby, B.C., and from his student days had expressed his desire to work for the Columbia Coast Mission, ("I slept with their pamphlet under my pillow," he says) but Dr. Vance of the Anglican College decreed that first he should serve in a city parish. He spent the required time initially in the Church of St. John the Divine in Maple Ridge (the oldest church in B.C.), then in St. Mary's Church in Vancouver's South Hill district, always waiting restlessly for a call to the mission. During his student years he had worked on a dairy farm in the United States, as whistle punk in a logging camp and as deckhand on a boat out of Whidbey Island. He believed that with this background he could communicate with the kind of people he would find up the coast.

Called at last to Quathiaski Cove and the *Rendezvous,* Venables threw himself into the work with enthusiasm, covering 7853 miles in 1937 and visiting 700 families. Church services, baptisms, marriages and burials added up to impressive figures. Even when he completed his route and the *Rendezvous* was tied up at Quathiaski Cove for a brief respite, emergency calls were apt to come in, anywhere from Whaletown to the Thurlow Islands, and he and Morton would head out once more, bidding farewell to domestic comforts.

"The Mission Ship answered emergency calls in all weathers and conveyed many indigent folk to and from hospital," Venables said in his report for 1937. "All weathers" included a time that winter, coming out of Bute Inlet by Stuart Island, when the *Rendezvous* took three big waves and emerged into Calm Channel covered with ice. In his ignorance of seamanship he set forth in storms that kept bigger boats tied up at dock, but Doug Morton, his able skipper and engineer, matched the chaplain in boldness and never refused to sail.

Venables, like Greene, played down the image of parish priest by wearing a sailor's cap and a heavy Indian sweater, the latter given to him by one of his Indian parishioners. "It was a lifesaver," he said of the sweater, which was used by several generations of his family. "Before I had it, I caught pneumonia going from the overheated hospital into the icy blast of a winter storm to get to the *Rendezvous*. When I lay ill in Quathiaski Cove, Mrs. Paine, a Seventh Day Adventist with a gift of compassion as large as her considerable avoir-dupois, insisted on sitting up all night with me, relieving my wife, and applying hot mustard plasters to my chest."[6]

Venables, who styles himself as "somewhat of a rebel", was determined to keep his services so simple that all denominations would be comfortable with them. Fortunately, Anglican services, ranging in form from High to Low Church practices, permitted clergy a wide choice while still conforming to the rules set out in the Book of Common Prayer. In an area where Seventh Day Adventists were predominant, Venables held the services on Saturdays. Harry Martin, an employee at the B.C. Packers' store at Quathiaski and a member of the United Church, told the chaplain that church meant most to him during Venables' day and that his church-going days ceased when the simple services came to an end.

A funeral service that Venables remembers with a sense of fulfillment was held one stormy day on the Rendezvous Islands. The coffin was made from an old, flat-bottom boat to which rope handles had been attached. Pelting rain had filled the open grave with several inches of water, and stones had to be carted from the beach to line the bottom before the coffin could be lowered. Only three or four families were living on the Rendezvous Islands at this time, but these had assembled for the service. Despite the steady downpour, the chaplain stood his ground, determined to give the little gathering the comfort and support that was needed. The day was November 11, and he brought his thoughts on Remembrance Day into the graveside service. "It is the service I like most to remember," he says.

Conveying patients to hospital often involved unantici-pated problems. In one lonely area they caught sight of a woman on the beach waving a tea towel. They anchored and went ashore in the dinghy, where they found the woman's husband delirious, sitting on his bed and apparently in great pain. Beside him on the table was a glass ball; the woman was a spiritualist and had been seeking advice from the spirits. The patient refused to lie down on the stretcher, so they were forced to strap him to a chair and then pack chair and man to the beach and into the dinghy. He was rowed out to the *Rendezvous* and lifted aboard, and they headed for the hospital.

The man had been a skipper on a sailing ship and in his delirium during the trip he shouted orders to an imaginary crew: "Step to starboard! Look alive, men! Draw the jib! Down staysail!", interspersing these with snatches of ribald songs that Morton feared would be embarrassing to the young chaplain. But Venables, despite his ingenuous appearance, had chosen to minister to this area where even educated lumber kings were apt to swear like troopers. He says he spoke in halls where beer bottles were hastily kicked under the seats before the sermon began, and showed no chagrin if loggers walked out when they had heard enough. As a result, he was always welcome. "Everyone liked him," says his engineer.

As was the case with most of the chaplains, Venables was unable to play the portable organ that had become an indispensable part of the mission services. A parishioner musically inclined was usually persuaded to man the organ, Mr. Tipton of Tipton's store being a willing performer when they called at Surge Narrows. On one occasion Tipton was unable to leave his store, so Morton carried the organ to the schoolhouse and essayed to play the hymns with two fingers. He had no inkling as to how many verses Venables would sing, but he watched the chaplain's mouth and whenever it opened he would start up his two-fingered accompaniment once again.

Apart from the ambulance service, and missionary and social service work, chaplains were expected to join in the lusty social hours of their parishioners to establish rapport. Morton helped out Venables at times. They hit Owen Bay on Sonora Island one evening when residents were holding their own version of a Major Bowes night (the original amateur programme where a gong was struck to order the summary removal of unsuccessful contestants.) Postmaster Logan Schibler was impersonating Major Bowes, and his daughter Helen acted as Master of Ceremonies for the little gathering. Morton contributed the old Whiffenpoof Song of Yale University:

"We're poor little lambs who have lost our way,
    Baa...baa...baa,
We're little black sheep that have gone astray,
    Baa...baa...baa..."

He got the gong.

Greene had been dubious of Venables' ability to follow the superintendent's original Santa act at Christmas parties, in which he stuffed the suit with inflated balloons for daring youngsters to pop. No doubt Greene's waggish humour was largely instrumental in producing its success, but the young chaplain was resolved to fulfill every requirement. He donned the old Santa suit, now threadbare and musty, always adding the traditional balloons. He recorded in *The Log* with wry humour his first Christmas visit to Squirrel Cove on Cortes, arriving there with a Christmas tree lashed to the mast head. The deck and rail of the *Rendezvous* were sheeted with ice and Venables, his arms filled with a bag of Christmas gifts, slipped on the deck and catapulted himself into the icy salt water. He came up wet and bedraggled, not to sympathetic concern but to gales of laughter from his heartless crew and the onlookers gathered on the shore. Undeterred, he changed his wet underwear for pyjamas, redonned his robes and manfully set out once more to distribute Christmas cheer.

Venables' further simplification of the church services to suit all believers, and his scheduling of them where possible to regular times in specified areas had led to a large increase in attendance. However, freedom to work and organize was curtailed by authority even here, and Greene's frequent absences and the resultant added areas Venables had to cover gave him little time to spend with his wife and children. When Alan Greene sold Sunset Cottage, which Venables was renting, the chaplain was unable to find another suitable house for his family. After three years of service, when the call came for him to take the church at Alert Bay and later to return to Victoria, he left the mission with a sadness tempered by the thought that he had realized a part of his youthful dream.

The *Rendezvous* was tied up throughout 1939 as no chaplain could be found to replace Venables. The filling of vacant parish positions was always a priority with the board. The Reverend J.D. Addison took over for a year in 1940, after which he joined the R.C.N.R. and the *Rendezvous* was laid up again until 1944.

3

Alan Greene returned to the west from his publicity campaign in the fall of 1936 to take charge of the *John Antle*, relieving the temporary substitute, the Reverend E.O. Robathan of Christ Church Cathedral in Victoria. Dr. Norman Jones from the Vancouver General Hospital filled in temporarily as physician, Wally Smith was still the engineer, substituting as skipper during Greene's absences, and Percy Cuttle was cook-deckhand. The ship was in need of an over-haul, and for the first time she was taken to Victoria, to the Victoria Machinery Depot, in the hope that Victoria citizens would become interested in her welfare.

Greene was finding the *John Antle*, the old *Florida V*, too slow and elderly to cover the routes of both ships (the *Rendezvous* being tied up for lack of crew) and she was having repeated breakdowns. She broke the crank-shaft of her main engine *en route* from Lasqueti Island to Squirrel Cove. Wally Smith, acting skipper, handled her through a stiff westerly up to Powell River and she was towed from there to Vancouver by the diesel tug *Progressive*. Off for a month, she returned to work only to have her main bearing run out, and she was towed back to Vancouver once again by tug. The necessity to make do with available ships in the stipulated price range was one reason for the constant changes. Bargain offers could not be overlooked, but they made for short life-times of service. Antle's "white elephant", the beautiful *Columbia* II, built to his specifications, was the exception, with 46 years of mission service.

Dr. Jones resigned after a year with the *John Antle* and his place was taken for five months in 1938 by Dr. W.N.M. Girling, an eye, ear, nose and throat specialist. These skills were utilized at once on his first trip and he was kept busy at every settlement and camp and in the Indian villages. One morning he had three tonsil operations scheduled, and found the anaesthetic mask had been forgotten. Wally Smith, the resourceful engineer, disappeared below and came up a short time later with an excellent mask he had constructed out of soldered copper wire, solving the crisis.

Dr. Ian MacKay, Dr. William Sloan, Dr. C. Wace and Dr. W.B. Clarke followed Dr. Girling for brief periods in 1938 and '39. Dr. Wace made a survey of the work of the *John Antle* and the *Columbia* while serving a few months on each, and presented his findings in a printed report to the Management Committee of the mission. Greene acted to correct several of the features he criticized.

The *John Antle* made an emergency trip in March 1939 to convey Mrs. Bertha Reedel of Coulter Bay on Cortes to the Campbell River hospital. This entailed a rough passage around Cape Mudge, never a comfortable experience and an ordeal for a young woman expecting her first baby at any moment. She says of the occasion: "I rode on the *John Antle* II to Campbell River one night in March, 1939, as my first child was due, and he was born at "Our Lady of Lourdes" hospital on the 21st March. It was a windy, rainy night and as the *John Antle* rounded Cape Mudge I felt very seasick. Sitting alone in the main lounge, I wondered what to do. We were broadside to the waves just then but I staggered out and leaned over the railing, drenched by spray, and lost my supper. I managed to return to my seat... in time to see a deckhand escorting the doctor outside as he was ill too! I wondered what help I would have had if my baby had made an entry into the world just then!"[7]

In the 1930s there were major changes on the *Columbia*. Engineer Cecil Fitzgerald resigned in 1936 after 12 years of service on the *Columbia*. Dr. R.W. Patten became ship's doctor, Dick French the engineer and J. Love the cook. The following year the crew changed again, with the exception of Dick French. Captain George MacDonald succeeded Captain Godfrey in October, Captain George Docherty having filled in for the summer before the turnover, and Major Hardinge of Victoria acted as lay chaplain.

Harold Auchinleck, who had worked as steward on the Canadian Pacific *Empress* boats before joining the mission, also began his long service as cook on the *Columbia* at this time. His short, chubby figure made him a natural choice for Santa on the Christmas cruises. Auchinleck amused the crew by turning out in immaculate attire with polished buttons and white cap when guests were expected aboard. The rest of the crew were casual in dress and "Auchie" as a result was sometimes mistaken by strangers for the *Columbia*'s captain. He was a shameless teller of tall tales, and the crew never knew when to take him seriously. Accepting one statement as gospel, Alan Greene introduced him to the Earl of Athlone as a cousin of Field Marshal Sir Claude Auchinleck during a royal visit to the ship.

Dr. G.E. Bayfield, an enthusiastic yachtsman, left his West Vancouver practice to replace Dr. Patten and spent two years, from 1937 to 1939 on the *Columbia*. He came honestly by his love of the sea; his grandfather was Admiral Henry W. Bayfield who charted Lake Ontario and the St. Lawrence River for the British navy after the War of 1812. Diversity marked the medical career of the doctor, a graduate in 1898 of the McGill medical school. He practised in Fernie, was superintendent of Vancouver General Hospital, a public health officer, doctor on a cruise ship to Australia, worked with the Northwest Mounted Police in the far north, and practised in Hyder, Alaska, in the Queen Charlotte Islands, and in Bella Coola.

While Dr. Bayfield was in Bella Coola, Ralph Edwards, the trumpeter swan conservationist, travelled down from his isolated ranch to ask for instructions on how to conduct the delivery of his wife in childbirth. The doctor persuaded him to bring her to the Bella Coola hospital, where their son was born, but the journey from Lonesome Lake, on foot over tortuous, rugged terrain, was so onerous that several years later Edwards delivered his daughter with the aid of a shelf of medical books.

Dr. Bayfield found plenty of the variety he desired during his stint as the *Columbia*'s surgeon. Besides medical treatment, he was expected to act as dentist and even as tree surgeon when settlers asked his advice on treating a diseased apple tree. He depended a good deal on preventive medicine and lectured parents and children on how to avoid sore throats. "Sore throat, sore throat, everybody in this place has a sore throat," he said, dreading an outbreak of diphtheria. (Penicillin was not yet available to the average doctor.) "An epidemic in these small places is something terrible. It's almost impossible to fight it. Everybody gets it."

The strenuous life on the *Columbia* appealed to him, though at the time he was in his 60s. A news article featuring him says: "He knows what it's like to climb down a 27–foot barnacle-encrusted ladder from ship to shore, for in the north the tides are enormous. He jumps across a great fender log, flashlight and satchel in hand, with the *Columbia* moving uneasily, as there is a strong sea running outside . . . He knows what it is, too, to answer an emergency call to some rockbound point and go ashore in an Indian canoe, water breaking over his oilskins. 'You have to be mighty careful in those things, they're liable to tip any minute,' he says."[8]

Dr. Bayfield recollected a stormy day when the *Columbia* called at Sayward, then a tiny, isolated settlement on the east coast of Vancouver Island. At the little store the doctor was told of a sick woman ten miles up the valley. He commandeered a car and sped off, with the car jumping and sliding along a flood-washed road, and muddy water dashing over the windshield. At his destination he had to walk through water up to his knees to reach the cottage of his patient. As he climbed aboard the *Columbia* after such visits, he would exclaim with enthusiasm, "A mighty interesting case. Mighty interesting."

In May 1939, the *Columbia* had *Vancouver Sun* reporter Charles Defieux aboard during her run. He kept a log of the trip, during which Dr. Bayfield was busy treating a variety of injuries and ailments. He taped up the broken ribs of a logger who met them in a gas-boat at Allison Harbour; at camps in

Nugent Sound he treated patients suffering from rib injury, acute neuralgia and toothache. The *Columbia* bucked the rapids to meet loggers who came *en masse* to exchange magazines at every stop. At Pine Island, too, the lightkeeper braved the ocean swells to row out to the ship for reading material. At floating homes, logging camps and Indian villages, Major Hardinge, the chaplain, visited his parishioners, magazines and books were distributed, the ailing and injured were treated, and several emergency cases were rushed to St. George's Hospital.

At Kingcome Inlet a party of 26 children came aboard from various outlying areas and were taken on a pre-arranged trip to Vancouver to see King George VI and Queen Elizabeth who were touring Canada. Mayor Telford welcomed them on their arrival in Vancouver. It was a good deed, and also good publicity for the mission. More publicity came with the visits in 1939 of Governor-General Lord Tweedsmuir and 1943 of Princess Alice and the Earl of Athlone to the flag-bedecked *Columbia*.

The ship helped out with some firefighting in July 1938. She was running down Loughborough Inlet when thick columns of smoke were sighted on the hillside behind the Fredricksons' small ranch. On the shore they saw Mrs. Fredrickson signalling urgently with a white cloth, while all around her dogs, cats, goats and other farm animals ran about in confusion, herded down to the beach to be away from the fire. The sea was too rough for the *Columbia* to come in close, but chaplain and steward went ashore in the rowboat, armed with pails and shovels. The closest source of water was half a mile away from the ranch, and a good deal of timber surrounded the property. The two men dug ditches to control the advance of the flames, battling for five hours before government rangers arrived to take over. The ground where they had worked was so hot that afterwards the cook and clergyman found their shoes were scorched and had to be discarded.

Although the staffing of the hospitals, churches and ships was a never-ending problem for Greene, as it had been for

Antle, a few grew to love the ships, their work, or their homes on the beautiful islands, and remained in harness for many years. Some were devout Anglicans who took part in the services and believed in the mission's spiritual as well as its practical work. Besides Antle and Greene, some of the long-term staff included chaplains Heber Greene and Rollo Boas, cook Harold Auchinleck, engineers Cecil Fitzgerald and Bob McCrea, and captains Ed Godfrey and George MacDonald. MacDonald served 19 years on the second *Columbia* and only retired when an accident on board cut short his days at sea. He was the son of William MacDonald, Vancouver alderman, and had been for many years with the B.C. Packers' fleet and West Vancouver ferries before joining the mission.

Captain MacDonald was married in 1938 to Mabel Lilian Tickell, formerly of London, England, with Alan Greene officiating. They made their home for the first two years in the *Columbia*'s home port, Alert Bay. The newlyweds had little time to themselves. Mabel would run to the garden gate when she heard the distinctive sound of the *Columbia*'s engine, but often the ship was answering an emergency call and Mac-Donald would take off his white cap and swing it against the ship's dark wood side, a signal that the expected weekend at home was cancelled. If all was well, he would wave both arms above his head and Mabel would hurry to the wharf to meet him. Even with the ship in port they usually found their hours of privacy invaded. Mabel was a pleasant, friendly woman and an excellent cook, and members of the crew, with little to entertain them in Alert Bay, invariably wandered over around dinnertime to "Mrs. Mac's" cottage on the waterfront.

During the war years the turnover of staff continued and increased alarmingly. At one point in 1939, Alan Greene was the sole missionary priest on the staff, covering the routes of the *John Antle* and the laid-up *Rendezvous*. For a time, when the Reverend J. Douglas Addison was skipper of the *Rendez-vous* in 1940, he also acted as her clergyman, cook, deckhand and engineer.

Dr. D.B. Ryall, who had served over seven years at St. George's Hospital, left in 1941 to join the R.C.A.F. Dr. Simpson, the *Columbia*'s doctor, took his place until Dr. Valentine St. John arrived as replacement. During this interval, a radio call came in for a doctor to attend a woman who had given birth to premature twins, so two nurses were dispatched on board the *Columbia*. The ship returned to Alert Bay with the twins, each of whom weighed just four pounds, and the grateful mother named them George and Richard after Captain George MacDonald and engineer Dick French of the *Columbia*.

As always, there were financial problems. The *John Antle* was desperate for funds for its medical service and for repairs. The ship needed $550 a month for running expenses and, unlike the *Columbia*, received no provincial grant. B.C. Packers helped out by writing off the remainder of the mortgage payments owed on her. By 1940 the *Columbia* was 30 years old and her wood hull was in need of extensive repair. Alan Greene hoped to raise $50,000 on his fundraising trips for an overhaul of the vessel, but this time he was unsuccessful. The beautiful flagship *Columbia* was still considered by many to be a luxury item with her graceful lines and her frequent hosting of celebrities. She required a crew of five to run her, and her staffing was increasingly difficult throughout the war. During the years 1939 to 1942 Doctors Bayfield, Wace, Worsley, Lang, Hamilton, Simpson, Dunn and Clark were among those serving successively as physicians on the *Columbia*, and cooks, deckhands and engineers came and went. The *Columbia* was criticized as ostentatious, and her critics cited the Roman Catholic missionaries who were travelling on the ferries or hitching rides on government or private boats.

Had they joined the *Columbia* on any of her runs, those who called her a social butterfly would have seen her in another light. In those hard times, the cost of ferrying coal by tug to St. Mary's and St. Michael's Hospitals was prohibitive. The *Columbia* carried five-ton lots to them, sacked, and every member of the crew fell to, slinging the sacks over their shoulders and packing them ashore. She visited over 100 logging camps on her patrol, plus making 100 more calls to isolated families and to communities ranging from Minstrel Island with seven or eight families, to Malcolm Island with a population of about 500.

May Ellingsen, wife of logger Elmer Ellingsen, says of this period: "The doctor from the mission ship came in to visit us at Phillips Arm and gave our pre-school children their immunization shots. This was much appreciated as it was quite an undertaking to get them all out to have it done in Campbell River, the nearest centre by then." St. Michael's, the old hospital built in 1911, had deteriorated badly and there was no money for repairs. The big logging companies had moved out, the hospital was deeply in debt, and in 1945 it was closed down. It was sold to sportsmen for a fishing lodge, and eventually abandoned.

One of the *Columbia*'s many ambulance missions occurred in 1942 when Captain Ralph Smith, skipper of the tug *Le Mars* contacted the *Columbia* by radio. The *Le Mars* was *en route* south from Ocean Falls and reported that her mate, John Gorton, was seriously ill with an acute chest condition. They expected to reach Christie Pass between six and seven p.m. Captain MacDonald was headed south from Alert Bay, having reached Boat Bay on Cracroft Island, but he turned about and headed north 56 miles to Christie Pass, the sheltered spot where they had arranged to meet. The *Columbia* got there an hour early, so she headed out into the rough waters of the sound to meet the tug. The *Le Mars* was coming along slowly with two big scows in tow. When they met, the *Columbia* drew alongside and 70-year-old Dr. Clark leapt like a movie stunt man from mission ship to tug. His bag was tossed after him, and he quickly examined and treated the sick man. The two vessels continued on to the calm waters of Christie Pass where the patient was transferred to the *Columbia* and taken to the hospital in Alert Bay.

4

In the spring of 1940, Alan Greene took a party in the *Columbia* to Kingcome for a conference with the Indians. The group included the Indian Agent, Mr. Todd; the Inspector of Indian Agencies in B.C., Mr. Coleman; Archbishop de Pencier; Ernest Halliday, pioneer settler at Kingcome; and F. Earl Anfield, principal of the Anglican Indian Residential School at Alert Bay.

They saw the new church, St. George's, built by the Indians in 1938 beside the mission house, and a tall Indian memorial totem pole erected in front of the house in memory of King George V. The oolichan run was on when the visitors arrived at the river, and sea lions and seagulls were gorging on the little fish that packed the water. The mission had ordered food for the group, and the Indians did the cooking for their guests. Inspector Coleman explained the duties of the agent and of the Indians, with Chief Scow interpreting for the elders. The older Indians were anxious to hold their dances again, explaining that there was no savagery involved. They also asked permission to give gifts after the dances; in short, they asked for the right to hold their potlatches again.

Through the years, the Indians had petitioned every possible source of aid in altering the law and permitting the resumption of their ancient dances, their traditional feasts and the distribution of gifts to establish rank. Back in 1929 an earnest appeal had been made to the Columbia Coast Mission. Four bands gathered at Kingcome to discuss the law with dignitaries of the church, and Chief Hubert Johnson assured the clergymen that the eating of human flesh at potlatches had always been a trick involving sleight of hand. However, the law remained on the statutes.

The Columbia Coast Mission maintained for the most part a paternal attitude towards the Indians. Alan Greene sided with many missionaries and educators who felt the potlatch prevented the educational, social and moral progress of the Indians. He agreed that many white customs displayed a "pomp and ceremony" akin to the ceremonial dances of the Indians and that the giving of gifts among the whites, if not as lavish as the potlatch distributions, was often excessive. On this perplexing question that roused so much controversy over the years, Greene, missing much of the profound meaning of the potlatch and the hereditary dances, hoped that a compromise could be found in some form of simple dance that might satisfy the older Indians.

The *Columbia* had always paid calls at Kingcome and always included a visit to postmaster Ernest Halliday on his 1000–acre ranch and farm at the head of the inlet. In summer and fall, visitors could marvel at the trees laden with fruit, plump cattle in the meadows and the thriving vegetable garden. Settlers came long distances by boat to buy produce from the Hallidays. The trip up the scenic inlet and the river was a delight in warm, calm weather but on the many cold, stormy days it was a punishing experience. Visitors might be held up several nights at the mouth of the river by rain and high winds, hearing the roar of the water as it dashed around the stumps and deadheads dotting the water. Crew and guests were happy to dry out at the Halliday farm where there was always a warm fire waiting and a big supply of dry house slippers on hand.

To reach the mission there was a further half-hour trip up the river in an open canoe, for the river was too shallow to take large boats. In bad weather they arrived at the mission soaked to the skin once again and shivering from the cold. Coming downriver presented problems at low tide as the river divided itself then into channels separated by sandbars. Sometimes even Greene was apt to choose the wrong channel and they were forced to backtrack or haul the canoe over the bars to find a channel leading to the river mouth. Archbishop Gower remembers such an occasion when, under protest, he was seated beneath an improvised canopy like an eastern potentate while the rest of the crew struggled to discover the right channel at two a.m. in pouring rain on a pitch-black night.

Two women missionaries, Miss Arrowsmith, teacher, and Miss Wakefield, nurse, were at Kingcome for seven years and were followed by the Misses Massey and Kirby. Reg Halliday, the son of the elder Hallidays, and Hillier Lansdowne, whose parents were the only other settlers in the area, were a great help along with the *Columbia*'s crew in solving the many problems of backwoods life for these women in the Indian village. Mr. and Mrs. Christmas, lay missionaries from Margo, Saskatchewan, arrived to take over at Kingcome in 1942 and continued the Halliday tradition of hospitality. Ernest Christmas taught in the Indian school, though he was not a qualified teacher, and Mrs. Christmas was the community nurse. To keep in constant touch with the Indians, they followed them to Glendale cannery in Knight Inlet the first year. The Indians spent the summers working in the cannery, which arranged that year to pay the missionaries for their medical services to the employees.

A visit to Kingcome village was a novel experience for many of the guests on the *Columbia*. Upriver they had to be carried piggyback at times when canoe or kicker grounded some distance from shore. An heroic sight was that of short, sturdy Alan Greene staggering manfully through the waves, bearing on his back the Bishop, Right Reverend Sir Francis Heathcote, who was six foot two.

Colonel H.T. Goodland, C.B., D.S.O., a member of the mission board, was a guest on the *Columbia* on one of her trips, and wrote a long newspaper article about his impressions, marvelling at the spectacular scenery of islands and fiords and describing the rescue work of the ship. His impression of Kingcome in the 1930s shows an outsider's viewpoint. He says in part:

"Kingcome Village was interesting in the extreme.... They had not had service in the village for some time, so one was held in the street with the congregation sitting on a porch or on the ground. The sermon, just a few hymns in English and in Indian, sung to the old tunes, and a few prayers. A few older women left their work of stripping blueberries from stalks and stewing them over an open fire in a shed, and strolled up and squatted on the ground opposite, regarding the proceedings in pagan silence and without any expression on their faces; whilst the totems also gazed woodenly at the sound of Christian hymns being sung by the descendents of the men who carved them."[9]

An even more unique experience was a visit to the Indian village of Gwyasdoms on Gilford Island, also on the *Colum-*

bia's route. Here people and animals moved slowly and calmly, untouched by the feverish bustle of city life. Huge dugout canoes were pulled up on the beach, and many other craft were moored around a large scow, selling clams to the scow's Indian manager. The clams were dug on the mudflats at night when the tide was low, and the lights of hundreds of gas lanterns set upon the flats by the diggers were a strange and lovely sight as they flickered in the darkness like distant stars.

Gwyasdoms was a very old village. The ruins of some of the big houses, occupied in the past, could still be seen. One huge house had been repaired and was used for conferences. The great windowless building, 75 by 36 feet, was constructed of cedar shakes and had the traditional earthen floor, roof open to the sky above the central fire, and a low sleeping platform running around the sides. Here, under the enigmatic gaze of giant winged totems, the missionaries talked to gatherings of Indians who squatted on the floor, wrapped in blankets. Only the younger generation of Indians spoke English. The mission's Christmas parties were held here, with a 15–foot, decorated Christmas tree lashed incongruously to one of the ancient totems.

A young intern from Vancouver General Hospital recorded his impression of an Indian village in 1940: a mysterious, barbaric scene to one fresh from a large, modern city. Dr. Harvey Hamilton spent a year with the *Columbia* from July 1940 to June 1941. He says he was treating a patient in Bull Harbour on Hope Island, that fogbound little island past the northern tip of Vancouver Island, where great waves roll in over the sandy shore. He was busily removing wax from his patient's ear when a call came from the Alert Bay wireless station. An Indian chief in a village 65 miles from Bull Harbour was seriously ill. The *Columbia* took off at once, reaching the village, probably Gwyasdoms, in the early evening.

An Indian youth paddled out to the ship in a dugout canoe and took the doctor ashore. He saw several houses and a few of the big community houses. He was led to one of these and taken to his patient who lay on blankets on a raised platform.

The yacht *Reverie,* sailed from England to Vancouver by Rev. John
Antle in 1939. (*Courtesy Ernest Antle*)

Mr. and Mrs. Ernest Halliday, pioneer homesteaders at Kingcome
from 1894. (*Courtesy C.G. Tuck*)

Edith Hansen married Harold Bendickson aboard the
Columbia, June 23, 1940, Rev. Alan Greene officiating. (*Courtesy Edith Bendickson*)

Cabin of second *Columbia* with portable altar set up for service, c.
1940. (*Courtesy Vancouver School of Theology*)

Dr. Harvey Hamilton aboard the *Columbia*, 1940. (*Courtesy Dr. Harvey Hamilton*)

Dr. Simpson performing a minor operation aboard *John Antle*, 1942. (*Courtesy Rev. Trefor Williams*)

L. to R. Rev. Gilbert Thompson, Harry Mason, Bob McCrea, Mrs. MacDonald, Mrs. G. Thompson, "Auchie", Capt. MacDonald at window, aboard *Columbia* Nov. 9, 1940, taking Mason to hospital in Vancouver. (*Courtesy Dr. Harvey Hamilton*)

Dr. M.D. McKichan examines patient at Thompson's camp, Von Donop Creek, 1940. Second *John Antle* in background. (*Courtesy C.G. Tuck*)

Ballenas Light Station, on the *John Antle*'s patrol. (*Courtesy C.G. Tuck*)

The second *Columbia*. (*Courtesy Vancouver School of Theology*)

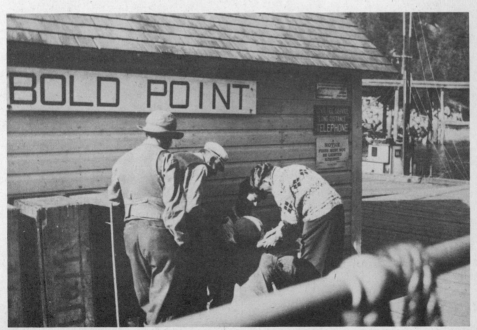

Dr. Gordon Worsley of the second *Columbia* examines a patient on
 Bold Point wharf, 1940. (*Courtesy C.G. Tuck*)

Visit to second *Columbia* of Earl and Countess of Athlone,
May 2, 1943. L. to R. Dean Swanson, Rev. Alan Greene,
Ben Drew, Archie De Land, Ronald Jackson, Capt. Mac-
Donald, W.P. Egerton, Bishop Sir Francis Heathcote, Dr.
Jeremiah Clarke, (ship's doctor), Bob McCrea, (engineer),
Sir Shuldam Redfern, Miss Grenfell, Capt. Leveson-Gower.
(*Courtesy Vancouver School of Theology*)

The Earl of Athlone, Capt. MacDonald, "Auchie", Rev. Alan
Greene, aboard second *Columbia,* 1943. (*Courtesy Vancouver
School of Theology*)

Rev. Alan Greene and the third
John Antle. (*Courtesy Alan
F. Greene*)

Church of His Presence, built
by Canon Alan Greene at
Redrooffs. (*Courtesy Rev.
Trefor Williams*)

Family of settlers on the *John Antle*'s patrol. (*Courtesy Alan F.
Greene*)

Rev. Rollo Boas and his family at the vicarage, Whaletown, Cortes
Island, c. 1946. (*Courtesy C.G. Tuck*)

Squirrel Cove church, also used as a school, burning down in 1948.
(*Courtesy C.G. Tuck*)

Kingcome Indian church and King George V memorial totem pole. (*Courtesy Rev. Trefor Williams*)

Mrs. MacDonald and Bingo aboard the second *Columbia*, c. 1946. (*Courtesy Mrs. G. MacDonald*)

The second *Columbia* aground on a reef in Warner Bay, Seymour Inlet, 1948. (*Courtesy C.G. Tuck*)

The *Gwa-yee,* with Kingcome Indian children, c. 1950. (*Courtesy C.G. Tuck*)

Ernest Christmas playing portable organ at Gwyasdoms, Gilford Island, c. 1950. (*Courtesy Alan F. Greene*)

By the flickering light of a lantern that cast strange shadows from the carvings of winged creatures on the houseposts, the doctor examined the sick chief. An Indian girl acted as interpreter for the old man, who refused to be taken away to the hospital. He wished to die there among his relatives, and during the night he passed away. On the *Columbia*'s next trip to the village, the crew saw that a memorial totem pole had been erected on a point near the village.

Harvey Hamilton was typical of many of the doctors, clergy or ship's crew who volunteered for mission work because of connections with the church, and who were therefore willing to accept the disadvantages of life at sea along with low pay. (Dr. Keith Wray-Johnston, at St. Mary's Hospital at this time, was also a licensed lay reader for the church.) Dr. Hamilton's father was a clergyman and his mother (who, alert and well, recently celebrated her 100th birthday) was a teacher for two years at the Indian residential school at Alert Bay.

The mission's yearly report for 1940 estimated that over a hundred logging camps, large and small, were visited by the *Columbia* when logging was in full swing, as well as over a hundred more points of call. A regular schedule was attempted, covering Seymour Inlet to Rock Bay, but emergency calls took precedence, so planned routes were often altered. Every six weeks, says Dr. Hamilton, the *Columbia* went to Vancouver and tied up for four or five days for repairs to the ship and a respite for the crew. When they arrived at the ship's home port of Alert Bay, Dr. Ryall usually had several operations scheduled at St. George's Hospital, and Dr. Hamilton was asked to assist.

He remembers the little floating homes on rafts up the inlets, many of them bright with window boxes of colourful flowers. The *Columbia* usually arrived in late afternoon and tied up to the float. Harold Auchinleck, the cook, would show a movie in the ship's cabin, and in the evening the crew would be asked into the float house for coffee. Here Captain MacDonald proved himself an inexhaustible source of information for the news-hungry family. Alan Greene was often away on fund-raising trips and it was the captain then who collected items of interest from loggers and settlers to pass on to other isolated homes on the route.

The *Columbia* called regularly up one inlet at a settler's cabin where a woman enjoyed poor health, though she suffered from no particular ailment. She took great pleasure in discussing her symptoms with the doctor, and had memorized complicated medical terms which she would reel off as she listed all her aches and pains and their various locations. As the *Columbia* approached the inlet, the crew would call out to MacDonald: "Well, Cap, are we going in to hear another organ recital?"

Coming down from calls in Seymour Inlet, the ship had to pass around a rocky little islet in the centre of a narrow neck of water, simple enough to navigate when timed for daylight and proper tidal conditions, but frightening at flood tide. They were far up one of the branching arms of the inlet when "Auchie" the cook complained of illness and pain. Dr. Hamilton diagnosed appendicitis and advised returning at once to Alert Bay. Captain MacDonald started off immediately, though it was dark and nearing flood tide. He had the reputation of being able to see in the dark, and to the relief of the crew he got the *Columbia* safely through the boiling water and back down the sound to the hospital at Alert Bay, where Auchinleck was operated on for acute appendicitis by Dr. Ryall, with Dr. Hamilton acting as anaesthetist.

Dr. Hamilton remembers an Indian wedding at Kingcome which he attended. The doctor was impressed by the fact that among all the very long speeches given at the wedding feast, none was given by the bridegroom. This was an ordeal he was soon to face himself at his imminent wedding in Vancouver to a nurse, the supervisor of the Eye, Ear, Nose and Throat Operating Room of the hospital where he had interned.

As the wedding day approached, Dr. Hamilton overheard plans of Dr. Ryall and the *Columbia*'s crew to give him a boisterous send-off at the dockside when he caught the Union Steamships boat at Alert Bay. He determined to outwit them. At three o'clock in the morning he collected his kit, crept from the *Columbia* and persuaded a fisherman to take him across the strait to Telegraph Cove, the next port of call of the steamer. The send-off party, ready on the Alert Bay wharf with noise makers and confetti, found their bird had flown.

It was agreed that Ernest Christmas at Kingcome should be provided with a boat, for many Indians had moved from Kingcome to Gwyasdoms on Gilford Island, this village being less remote and offering remunerative work in the sale of clams for the white market. Without transportation, Christmas had no means of visiting them frequently. Also, there was no school or church at Gwyasdoms and some form of assistance was needed. Miss O'Brien resigned from her post at Village Island in 1945 so this reserve would require visits from the Christmases as well. After a two-hour discussion between Bishop Heathcote, Alan Greene and Christmas regarding pros and cons, it was decided in 1945 to supply Kingcome mission with a small launch.

The *Bob* was found, bought in 1945 and renamed *Gwa-yee*, the Kwakwala word for "inside place", referring to Kingcome. She was 28 feet long, with a seven-by-eight foot cabin containing a double bunk in the fore-peak, and fitted with a four-cylinder, 18-h.p. engine. She was in service for eight years, with Kingcome as her headquarters. A one-dollar licence had to be bought at the time she was acquired, permitting her to use gas for her engine, as gas was rationed during the war years.

Ernest Christmas brought the *Gwa-yee* home in a wild southeaster storm. Lashed with rain throughout the journey, Christmas and his wife arrived at Kingcome to find the river full of new snags. Evading these, they got to the mission only to discover the raging waters had overflowed their banks and surged up to cover the third step of the house.

Living in this beautiful area had its unpleasant aspects, as floods occurred regularly in spring and fall. The *Gwa-yee* was trapped in ice one year and had to be hauled out to prevent her from being crushed when the breakup came. Another year, the ice breakup carried away skiffs, canoes and gasboats that were shoved along by the weight of the moving floes. Christmas and young Adam Dick fell through the ice as they tried to launch a canoe to rescue a skiff. They were forced to change their soaking wet clothes three times before all the boats were safely docked at nightfall.

5

Hard times continued for the ships and for many of those they served. In 1941, 74-year-old Carl Halverson came aboard the *John Antle* to be treated for painful muscles. He was a hand troller, and told the crew that two days of rowing had got him only one 4½-pound salmon, for which he was paid 15¢. Settlers struggled to make ends meet, some with ingenuity. Student-chaplain Roland Hill on the *John Antle* wrote in 1941 of a visit to Egmont, where Mr. and Mrs. Blakeley had made themselves a small garden on their rocky property by bringing soil, pailful by pailful, from the mainland to create a few productive beds. In these they grew four crops: tulips in the spring, potatoes in summer, tomatoes in the fall and cabbages in December.

The *John Antle* was desperate for funds for medical expenses, running expenses and repairs. A petition for an annual grant for upkeep was refused by the provincial government. Auguring changes to come, Canadian Airways (later absorbed by Canadian Pacific Airlines) had begun bush flying in northern B.C. with Russell Baker as pilot in 1938. A weekly service by Canadian Airways between Vancouver and Zeballos on the west coast of Vancouver Island, and one between Vancouver and Seymour Inlet with way stops *en route* also started up that year. Injured loggers in these areas could now be flown out by plane. Yet the mission boats were still of great value. Camps in places inaccessible to planes were dependent on boat travel.

One of the many war-time problems of the ships was the ruling of naval authorities forbidding the *Columbia* to acknowledge her S.O.S. calls. Later this ruling was amended, allowing her to acknowledge calls but forbidding her to give her location. The *John Antle* made regular calls during the war at the army base on tiny York Island, and Alan Greene spent several days each month there as chaplain for the Coastal Defense Unit stationed on York.

The wedding on the *Columbia* in 1940 of Edith Hansen to Harold Bendickson was a happy interlude. The flag-bedecked ship docked at Port Neville and bride, bridesmaids and flower-girl in their high heels and floor-length dresses climbed up the gangplank to the *Columbia* whose chapel was packed tight with over 100 guests. Setting forth on their honeymoon in the groom's boat, the *Sea Pal*, the couple had first to head out into the roughest part of the choppy waters to report to the navy boats from York Island Army Base that were patrolling Johnstone Strait.

Many doctors were serving overseas during the war, and the shortage was acute. Others preferred to work in comfort in the cities where there was also a shortage. Some elderly doctors who came out of retirement to help fill the gaps on the mission boats were unable to stand up to the rugged conditions and their terms of service were brief. A sad event for the *John Antle* occurred during the winter of 1942 when Dr. W.A. McTavish, after a strenuous snowball fight, started the walk up to St. Michael's Hospital and collapsed and died on the trail. Captain Wally Smith and engineer John van der Est brought the body to Vancouver and the doctor was given a burial at sea. His ashes were scattered on the waters of Welcome Pass from the stern of the *John Antle* by Alan Greene.

C.H. Fitzgerald, father of engineer Cecil Fitzgerald, died in 1940. He had served with Alan Greene for four winters on the *Rendezvous,* and fished and worked as a guide during the summers. Greene remembered him as always good-natured, never complaining as he struggled up beach and cliff in deep snow, burdened with the 32-pound organ and other paraphernalia at the various stops, and with only the light of a flashlight to guide him. He would heat two bricks, wrap them in newspapers and slip them into the bunks as excellent substitutes for hot water bottles for Greene and himself on cold nights at sea.

Cecil Fitzgerald remembers back in 1912 when Alan Greene

would call at Campbell River and Cecil as a small boy would be told to pack the portable organ back to the *Eirene* after a concert while his father and Greene strolled ahead. He felt this was very hard lines, as it was a heavy load for a youngster.

Captain Wally Smith resigned in 1942 after eight years on the second *John Antle*. He had been with her since the mission acquired her, in the capacity of engineer and captain. Alan Greene took over as skipper after Smith left. The *John Antle* promptly burned out her bearings and was out of commission for a time. The *Rendezvous,* tied up after J.D. Addison joined the navy, was used to cover the *John Antle*'s patrol while she was out of service, and Dr. Simpson, substituting on the *Columbia*, shifted to the *John Antle* as doctor and engineer. The switching, substituting, and tie-up of vessels due to lack of crews was a constant headache for the superintendent.

In 1944 something new was tried out: a woman doctor. Dr. Florence Nichols had enjoyed an earlier visit to the west and returned seven years later to visit friends in Bella Coola. She was offered a ride as far as Alert Bay on the *Columbia*, after which she could transfer to a Union Steamships boat. At the Pender Harbour stop she went ashore to look over St. Mary's Hospital and was deeply moved by the plight of the nurses there who had no doctor on the staff. The *Columbia*'s Dr. Dunn had transferred to Queen's Hospital and the ship was without a doctor in August. Dr. Nichols offered her services for September to Greene, who hesitated at first, unable to visualize acceptance of a woman doctor by his "timber beasts." But she persuaded him to take her on for five weeks, with Dr. Dunn available for consultation at Alert Bay. She borrowed medical books from Dr. Taylor's large library at St. Michael's Hospital (soon to close) and joined the *Columbia* on the ship's first trip made with new, more advanced radio-telephone equipment. This allowed direct communication with logging camps that had similar phones in use and also gave immediate long-distance communication with the head office in Vancouver.

Two calls came in at once, one for the chaplain at a wedding at Blind Channel, and one for the doctor at Dumaresq

Camp in Seymour Inlet. They decided to call early for the wedding and speed it up so both calls could be answered. It was one of many new experiences for the eastern doctor. The bride arrived and climbed aboard, the phonograph playing "Here Comes the Bride" as she descended the stairs to the chapel. The *Rodney I* was docked beside the *Columbia* and her skipper decided to attend the ceremony, considerately kicking off his boots before entering the cabin. The easterner was horrified to see a guest enter "church" in his stocking feet, but soon realized standards differed here. The gramophone played the Wedding March as the bride departed, and the *Columbia* took off for Dumaresq Camp.

Bob McCrea, formerly of the tug *La Reine*, had replaced Dick French as engineer. He remembers going to the doctor's cabin after the ship's movie to ask her to come and have a "mug up" (boat slang for a coffee break.) Her startled reaction was later explained. She thought it must mean "spooning". Harold Auchinleck, the cook, delighted in teasing the doctor, who was never sure if he was serious or not when he told her the paint scraper was the captain's razor, that water towers were lookouts to sight wild Indians, that clams were hunted with guns, and that whales ducked under the float houses to scrape barnacles off their backs. Actually, this last story was fact rather than fiction, as in 1948 the *Columbia* called at Belleisle Sound, off Kingcome Inlet, and found the logging camp there had been bothered by whales coming under the floats to rub their backs. They were blowing constantly, emitting a nauseating odour, and the loggers' wives persuaded the men to move camp to the farther shore. This area was in deep shade, however, and they chose a lesser evil and moved back to the pleasant sunshine and the temporary annoyance of the whales.

At Glendale and Bones Bay canneries, Dr. Nichols innoculated 63 Indian children against diphtheria, with Heber Greene and "Auchie" helping her by swabbing arms and keeping records. "A few kids howled," wrote Heber. Auchinleck showed a movie to cheer the small patients after their ordeal, and the chaplain managed to fit in three baptisms.

Dr. Nichols found she was expected to act as dentist as well as doctor in the outlying areas. On one occasion she struggled for five or ten minutes to get a good grip on the upper back molar of an Indian patient, and in the midst of her perspiring efforts to extract the tooth a second Indian nervously waiting his turn got up muttering, "Thank you very much. I think I'll see a dentist," and departed.

The expected resistance was there, but she managed to prove herself to patients and mission. At one stop, old Lars Aas came aboard and Harold Auchinleck introduced him to the young woman: "This is our doctor." After a startled double take, Lars said gamely, "Well, we're lucky to have any kind of doctor these days." Just before they pulled out, he came back to ask, "I know you're a human doctor, but I wonder if you would see my dog?" Far from feeling offended, Dr. Nichols said she felt complimented, having learned that the dog was his dearest possession. The crew seized on the incident with delight as one more chance to tease her. "The truth is out," they said. "We knew you were a horse doctor all the time."

In the hospital one day she treated a young man who seemed reluctant at first to let her examine his ugly chest wound. When she checked up on him the following day he greeted her cheerfully. "I nearly bolted when I saw a woman doctor," he confessed, "but I decided you looked very intelligent."

6

A happy addition to the mission staff was Alan's older brother, Heber Greene, who joined in 1942 and was chaplain of the *Columbia* for 16 years. Heber Greene was a diligent, warm-hearted priest with a tremendous interest in people. Alan Greene suggested the letters "P.P." should be added to his titles, for "Peripatetic Priest", as he made a habit of going ashore at various stops, particularly on the northern end of Vancouver Island. He would arrange to rejoin the ship at some point, but would become so absorbed as he hiked about, discovering isolated camps, visiting settlements and reserves and becoming familiar with the problems of the people, that the *Columbia* would wait for him in vain.

"Heber Hunting" became a year-long game of the *Columbia*'s crew as the men tried to guess where he might turn up to be collected aboard again. On one occasion he went ashore to the Indian village at Port Hardy, telling them to wait, but was inspired to continue on down to Coal Harbour in Holberg Inlet. The crew of the *Columbia* were unable to find him in Port Hardy and were about to sail with the tide when Heber roared up just in time in a car driven by one of his parishioners, a Mr. Cadwallader. Before he went aboard, Heber buried Peter Pascaro of the Indian village, "after which his house and contents were burnt up in Indian fashion."[10]

Like his brother Alan, one year his junior, Heber was a graduate of the University of Toronto and of Wycliffe College. He had gone to the Queen Charlotte Islands in 1914 as missionary in Old Masset and was ordained there the same year in the Indian church that was built in 1888, the year of his birth. He served at St. Paul's in Masset the following year and then went overseas for three years as chaplain to the 7th Brigade in France. Returning to British Columbia, he served in Squamish, Mission, Agassiz and Hope before joining the Columbia Coast Mission at the age of 55. Enthusiastic, loving, unpretentious, he was an ideal priest.

Overshadowed by his younger brother, the colourful promoter, Heber's influence was deeper than many might suspect. The Reverend Eric Powell says it was working with Heber on the *Columbia* and recognizing his genuine goodness that inspired him to enter the priesthood. When he was in charge of the Powell River parish, a young man came to him saying he wanted to be married in the church. Powell was astounded, as the prospective groom had been known throughout his adolescence as the "tough boy" of the town, who would never set foot in a church. "What makes you want to be married in a church?" Powell asked. "Well," was the answer, "a good old guy off the mission boat baptized me and I'd like to be married in his church." The good old guy was Heber.

One of Heber Greene's first trips on the *Columbia* was to

Sointula on Malcolm Island, to officiate at a Finnish wedding. The Finnish settlement had been founded in 1901 when the socialist author, editor and playwright Matti Kurikka led a party of Finns there to found a Utopian colony where "a high cultural life would be built, away from churches that destroy peace, away from all the evils of the outside world." Heber found them much less hostile than in the past (a United Churchman had once been thrown into the sea.) One man asked him if he really believed in what he was doing, and the chaplain answered that if he didn't he would be a camp flunkey as he'd be paid just as much in that job. This disarmed the Finn and they had a good laugh together.

The *Columbia* called weekly at Sointula and the doctor examined and treated the children. Gifts of produce were often handed over to the mission ships, usually by settlers of other nationalities who had come to Malcolm Island after the tragic failure of the Utopian venture. Greene liked to drop in at the home of Ole Olsen who ran a prosperous farm and owned an old horse that was always on view in the meadow. On one occasion Olsen came down to the wharf and invited Greene to dinner. During the generous repast the chaplain remarked, "By the way, where's your old horse? I don't see him out there." "You're eating him, preacher," came the placid reply.

Heber was a diabetic, with a craving for sweets. Archbishop Gower remembers days when crew and clergy were crowded around the *Columbia*'s small table during a meal, and as they chatted, Heber's hand would stray involuntarily towards the bowl of sugar cubes. A shout from the crew would arrest the movement and Heber would give an apologetic grin. The cook was adamant in his refusal to allow the chaplain sweets in his diet. The old priest delighted in outwitting him and once went to several houses, begging a cookie from each one. The *Columbia* was unable to sail until he returned, and by that time the tide was out. The ship had to be shoved off the sandbank by deckhand Powell and the cook while Heber sat on deck happily munching his cookies in wicked defiance.

Like his brother Alan, Heber possessed both enthusiasm and energy. In his case the energy was most apparent in his many hikes about the country, visiting communities for longer periods than the *Columbia's* scheduled stops would allow, but unlike Alan who prided himself on dancing with the settlers until parties broke up around three a.m. or later, Heber was apt to weaken early. At one dance, a very husky Indian woman came up to him, announcing, "Come along, old sport, you're my pick." She was tireless, still whirling him about after 20 minutes, and no other woman responded to his appealing glances by "tapping" him to cut in. At 11 p.m. he pleaded a need for sleep before an early rising and escaped, exhausted.

Heber was always deeply interested in the problems and welfare of the Indians. He went out of his way to ensure equal advantages in medical care for both Indian and whites. Learning that an Indian boy at Alert Bay was seriously ill with peritonitis, he called in Squadron Leader Christie of the R.C.A.F. hospital at Hardy Bay to consult with the doctor at St. George's. In another case, after receiving permission from the Indian Agent, he arranged to have an Indian woman transferred to the Hardy Bay hospital as she was anxious to be near her own people in that area during her operation. Criticism of Indians irked him; he answered it by pointing out that there were as many dishonest or drunken whites as Indians, and that the Indians showed steady improvement in housing and education.

He worked on a card index of the white and Indian population covered on the *Columbia's* route. Bringing the Indian index up to date was a momentous task. He recorded one Indian family at Fort Rupert that went down to great-great grandchildren, with branches of the family reaching out in all directions. Tracking them down was a problem, as the families left their villages to go fishing, trapping and clam digging. Gwyasdoms village on Gilford emptied when they followed the oolichan run up the inlet.

Heber made a point of attending meetings of the Native Brotherhood of B.C. and discussing problems with the Indians and the Indian Agent, particularly the desire of the natives for changes in the Indian Act. He studied the paintings of Emily Carr after visiting Blunden Harbour and felt they helped him to understand the Indian point of view. He said that when he spoke against some of the Indian habits they would answer, "White man does it." He decided it was logical that if the white man shared their faults, they should share in his privileges. Returning from watching a football game at Cape Mudge between Alert Bay and the cape Indians, he travelled back to Alert Bay on a seiner with another passenger, the well-known Haida Indian missionary, the Reverend Peter Kelly of the United Church boat *Thomas Crosby*, and seized the occasion to be well briefed on Indian affairs.

Heber Greene never hesitated to tell a joke on himself. He held a Sunday School class on Minstrel Island during his travels, and congratulated himself on successfully inspiring the youngsters with high ideals. As the class was dismissed he heard one boy say in a tone of relief, "Now let's play poker!" Another small boy in one of the logging camps always greeted him with "Hi, Hallowe'en!" The chaplain wondered if the child thought he looked like a Hallowe'en pumpkin, but the mother finally decided the greeting resulted from the youngster hearing the men call out, "Hallo, Greene!"

When he was visiting a logging camp by Drury Inlet, one of the loggers decided to play a fast one on the men in the bunkhouse. Rushing in, he shouted, "The show's on!" and there was a speedy exodus to the *Columbia* in anticipation of a movie. Faces fell comically when they found the chaplain in the midst of a service. "However," said Greene, "they were good sports and stayed on."

Loggers considered their bunkhouses their home and retreat and were apt to resent a sermon forced upon them. Greene was given permission by the foreman to speak in one bunkhouse and was leading the men in a hymn when a group of dissident loggers who had gathered in the adjoining bunkhouse drowned out the hymn by shouting songs from the Communist Song Book. Greene went over and congratulated them on their singing and on getting a bigger turnout than his.

His reaction was a surprise to them and his cheerful good humour hard to resist. They never repeated the heckling.

He found it amusing when his doctor, just out of the army, prescribed exercise and physical "jerks" to cut down his increasing weight. He had just returned from the Drury Inlet visit, during which he was told that a doctor was needed up the lagoon. Directions to reach the patient were: "See that trail? Follow it until you hit the lagoon and you'll find a boat—probably." Greene and the ship's doctor traced the snow-covered trail through the woods with difficulty, found the boat and rowed a long way up the lagoon until they came to a log boom. Both men shouted, and eventually a woman appeared in a small boat and rowed over to them to be examined. Greene had lost five pounds by the time he got back to the *Columbia*, and felt that more exercise was the last thing he needed.

When he visited Lasqueti Island he hiked over 32 miles of road, seeing 50 of the 54 families and encountering "everything from atheists to Fundamentalists and all shades of opinions in between." His attempts to bring sheep to the Anglican fold were countered by arguments from atheists, agnostics, United Church members, Roman Catholics, Jehovah's Witnesses, Seventh Day Adventists, Mormons and converts to Father Divine. The Pentecostal Church, offering informality and excitement in its services, had a mission at the north end of Vancouver Island from 1951 on, and its influence was felt in Alert Bay and the Indian villages on nearby islands. At Port Hardy, Heber shared a hotel room with a drunken logger who railed against religion half the night before he fell asleep and allowed the weary missionary to enjoy a few hours of rest.

On one of his many trips on foot around northern Vancouver Island, Greene hiked five miles to the airport at Fort Rupert and was about to continue on to the Indian villages. The local authorities persuaded him to wait and spend the night as it was growing late. They made up a bed for him in the old R.C.A.F. jail. Heber remembered a story his mother had told him about his christening. His given names were

Heber Harrington after two famous Anglican bishops. "Wouldn't it be awful," his mother had exclaimed after the ceremony, "if with such names he should ever land in jail!"

By boat, on foot, on logging speeders, Heber Greene travelled about the country, holding services, baptizing infants, and arranging for social assistance for the needy and medical care for the sick. "Boarded the speeder for Nimpkish Lake," he wrote in *The Log,* "where I caught the mail boat, but not before helping to load sacks." He failed to convert many loggers but he won the respect of hard-working men. A mechanic up the coast was called to repair the ship's toilet, an unpleasant job in which he was forced to wind his arms and legs around it to get a tool-hold on the rusted nuts. "How much do we owe you?" he was asked as he completed the job. "Hell!" roared the mechanic. "Do you think I'd soak the God-damned mission? Forget it!"

7

Towards the close of the war years, in 1944, Rollo Boas joined the mission and was skipper and chaplain on the *Rendezvous* for ten years, with headquarters at Whaletown on Cortes Island. Born in Regina, Saskatchewan in 1910, Boas received his B.A. degree at the University of Manitoba and went on to its affiliate, St. John's College, for his theological degree. Before joining the mission he served in the Dioceses of Ruperts Land and Edmonton. He was most deeply interested in the spreading of the Anglican faith among his British Columbia parishioners, but he is remembered more widely as the builder of the medical and dental clinic at Whaletown.

The chaplain was aided in his parish work for a time by lay reader John Maunsell on Cortes, and by lay preacher and teacher Doris Lancaster who conducted a vacation school for children in the Egmont area, rowing from one island to another. Sometimes the young woman had to be rescued as she battled the waves in stormy weather, and reached her destination towed by a friendly fisherman.

"Had I gone to a foreign country I could hardly have expected many more changes and new things," Boas said.[11] Coming from the interior, he was as bewildered as Alan Greene had been back in 1911 with logging and nautical terms. Loggers spoke casually of donkeys, cats, corked boots and widow-makers, and boatmen too used a language that was like a foreign tongue to him. He was struggling to tie a clove hitch at one time, and a sea constable, watching the result which came out upside down, was moved to ask, "Tell me, how long have you been to sea?" Alan Greene advised him: "Read your tide book as often as your Bible," after Boas anchored the *Rendezvous* too close to shore and the outgoing tide left her stranded 25 feet from the water.

His first taste of rough Bute weather came on a trip up the Homathko River at the head of Bute Inlet. The tide was dead low, and snags could be seen sticking up in the inlet and in the river. The *Rendezvous* grounded on the bottom, and though Boas shoved her off, he was unable to restart the engine. The Reverend Kendall was with him and as they drifted helplessly Kendall caught at one of the snags and held on to it until the rising water covered it and he was forced to relinquish his hold. Once more they were at the mercy of wind and waves. Luck was with them, however, for a logger came by, towed the *Rendezvous* to safety, and took the priests upriver in his shallow gas-boat. At the Indian village they had come to visit, they saw a hydroplane and helicopter by the shore, another sign of the changing times that would eventually put an end to the mission fleet.

Boas had 20 communities to visit on his route of over 500 miles, and called in as well at small cabins in the woods, taking messages out from isolated settlers, following the tradition of earlier chaplains. The parents of Constable Ennals at Campbell River gave him eight records of Christmas carols, and he took these with him on his Christmas cruises. Anchoring in little coves, he would put the record player on top of the cabin and let the sound of the music echo across the water. At Owen Bay, children gathered on the wharf to sing along with the carols.

Mrs. Boas, the former Kathleen Mary Harrington, had been a practising dental nurse, and travelled with her husband when he ferried patients to the hospital. Their two young daughters often came with them, keeping up their studies by correspondence. The medical and dental clinic established by Boas was held twice a month, with Dr. Bathurst Hall and Dr. Phillip Margetts coming every second Friday from Campbell River to Heriot Bay by water and land taxi and being ferried from there to Whaletown in the *Rendezvous*. The clinic was held first in the vicarage, with the doctor's office in the unfinished quarters upstairs, and the dentist setting up his chair in the children's bedroom. On one occasion when there was a smallpox scare, 108 patients were vaccinated in one day, coming and going through the family quarters in a steady stream. A separate building for the clinic was opened on November 8, 1951, and after John Antle's death it was renamed the John Antle Memorial Clinic. Doctors Hall, Depew, Maloney and Harris took turns coming from Campbell River to man the clinic.

Boas in 1944 said "the Holy Catholic faith and teaching alone can fulfill the plan of Christ" [12] but by 1953 he was resigned to the fact that few coast dwellers were Anglicans and services must necessarily be simple to avoid conflict with a variety of Christian beliefs. He built churches on Cortes where there was a demand, however small: St. Saviour's-by-the-Sea at Cortes Bay and St. John the Baptist at Whaletown.

Boas believed the large congregations of Anglicans and the impressive services found in city churches were necessary for inspirational renewal, and he was grateful when his work took him to Vancouver and he could attend a service there. He took pride in the furnishings of the altar on his little launch, and wrote: "We have a Trinity green frontal, fair linen cloth, oaken cross, and the needed vessels of the church's altar." He was more comfortable with established city congregations, or the little pockets of sympathizers up and down the coast. Loggers were hard nuts to crack, and most of them thrived on dialectics. "Sometimes," Boas wrote, "in sheer fatigue, we head for a bay, a home, where we do know there will be no arguments, no doubts and no whys."[13]

Many settlers as well as loggers were inclined towards skepticism. A free-thinking postmaster on Quadra Island welcomed Alan Greene's visits with genuine pleasure. "We always have great arguments," he commented with satisfaction. And not all loggers could be lumped together as unbelievers and aggressive alcoholics. Many logging families kept up a close connection with the church. Even in the early days, Antle spoke proudly of one of the camps as "the sober camp." He described foreman Sol Ramey of Hastings Mill Company as "tall and powerful, unlike most of his contemporaries no drinker." Operators like Frank Gagne who logged for many years on the coast, discouraged drinking among his men for financial as well as moral reasons; it lowered the work capacity. Gagne brought his men to church and to local functions and good behaviour was the norm.

To quote Antle again: "One of the things that impressed me most in the old-time camps was the respect given to the child. Hard swearing and rough among themselves, the presence of a child muted the swearing and brought out an unsuspected gentleness, which quelled forever in me that one-sided view of the logger obtained in the city, where every device to empty his pockets and debase his nature is practised by his so-called friends."[14] Most chaplains closed their eyes to moderate drinking; few Anglicans are teetotalers. But men who drank heavily and steadily as their only recreation after hard, dangerous work in the woods resented the missionaries of many persuasions who tried to wean them from a practice promising them a few hours of euphoria.

8

The last years of the war saw one of the worst doctor shortages in the northern area. Most able-bodied doctors had joined the forces. During Heber Greene's first years with the *Columbia*, the ship was staffed in turn by Doctors Simpson, Clark, Dunn and Gibson. Pte. Marian Gray, studying to get her M.D. at Toronto, filled in for a short time on the hospital ship. The *Columbia* fouled her propeller on a submerged log in 1944 and after a slow run to Vancouver was tied up for two weeks. During the lay-off, Dr. Gibson went home to North Pender Island where he suffered a stroke and died. There was no replacement for him when the *Columbia* was ready to sail, and she was used only for emergency runs.

Although plagued with doctor shortages, the *Columbia* was fortunate in her long-service cook and captain. Harold Auchinleck, who had rejoined the *Columbia* in 1941 after a long illness, stayed with the ship as cook until he reached 70 years of age. Captain MacDonald served 19 years. In his later years, MacDonald became a staunch, crusty old sailor, given to outspoken comments and autocratic decisions. He was troubled by stomach ulcers, and often in the midst of a fierce storm the violent sounding of the bell brought Powell, the deckhand, on the run. The trip from galley to wheelhouse had to be made along the outside deck, and Powell would stagger and skid over the heaving, sleet-covered deck, precariously balancing the captain's daily glass of soothing eggnog.

A certain clergyman was in the habit of asking for handouts from the ship if his own food supplies ran short. Whenever they sailed south and approached that particular port, Mac-Donald would roar, "Lock up the galley! There he is on the float, waiting to rob us!"

In the final year of the war, the second *John Antle* was put up for sale. Lack of money to cover running expenses and repairs, and the difficulty of supplying her with a full crew made it imperative to find a smaller boat that Alan Greene could run unassisted. She was sold to Ranta, Salo and Ranta of Port Angeles for use as a tuna-fishing vessel. As the new owners prepared to leave with her, the main circulating pump broke down and one final expense for the mission was $150 to replace it.

Features of the third *John Antle* allowed her to be managed by one man if necessary. The pilothouse ran clear across the ship's beam, with narrow decks outside, and was streamlined forward and aft, with large plate glass windows all around. A searchlight and electric air whistle had been installed, and the steering wheel and engine controls were easily operated by the skipper. The pilothouse cabin was large enough to serve as a small chapel and the chart table would accommodate the ship's altar. The cabin aft, furnished as kitchen and dinette, had a small office aft of it with radio-telephone, the radio having loud-speakers both in the cabin and the pilothouse, so incoming messages could be heard by the man at the wheel.

The ship was built in 1932 by Vancouver Shipyards for Arthur Falkland and Howard Head of Cobble Hill on Vancouver Island, and was christened the *Panda*. She had been run very little by the owners during the war due to gas restrictions, and in 1942 had been chartered to the R.C.A.F. who nicknamed her the *Goose*. She was redesigned for the mission by Gilbert Jukes of Vancouver Shipyards.

At the start, Alan Greene as skipper-engineer ran her with the Reverend Lorin A.C. Smith as deckhand and 15-year-old John Preston as cook. Dr. Simpson served briefly until he was needed at St. George's Hospital. Pender Harbour was the base, and the area concentrated on included Lasqueti, Texada, Hardy, Nelson and Thormanby Islands and all of Jervis Inlet. Greene planned to circle the whole missionary area from time to time in his capacity as superintendent.

The third *John Antle* served the Columbia Coast Mission for 12 years, changing her name to *Laverock II* for her last two years with the mission.

Chapter Five

Changing Times and Needs

I

St. George's Hospital in Alert Bay was desperate, making do with a succession of relief doctors who changed at frequent intervals. Dr. Simpson, Dr. Rolston of Victoria and Drs. Stevenson and Kelly of St. Paul's Hospital, Vancouver, were among those who filled the gap briefly. Alan Greene was unable to find the two permanent doctors essential for the adequate running of the hospital, despite co-operation from the College of Physicians and Surgeons in Vancouver and the Medical Procurement and Assignment Board in Ottawa. He had approached the Indian Affairs Branch in Ottawa with the proposal that they assume the running of the hospital, without success.

In 1947, after 40 years of service by the mission, the management was taken over by the St. George's Hospital Society, run by a local board representing the larger logging interests, the community of Alert Bay and the Department of Indian Affairs. The building was leased to the society, which later used it as a nurses' home. A former R.C.A.F. 60-bed hospital in Port Hardy was then towed down the 30 miles in 16 separate sections and set up behind the old St. George's building. The *Columbia* planned to continue her medical, social and evangelical work in the area, but St. Mary's was now the only mission hospital.

Antle, who had put the crying need for medical service in the north at the top of his priorities, could see his accomplishments during his years in the mission. Alan Greene, in the late 1940s, witnessed the closing down of hospitals and the start of the plane services that would eventually supplant the mission ships. His prime interest was thus the spiritual side of the work, and in these northern areas the disinterest of many was disheartening. Radical western thought was also alarming to an eastern conservative. Said Greene in his pamphlet, *Scattered Sheep*: "The men are, in many camps, largely Scandinavian, and from those countries has come a spirit of radical socialism that is far from being sane or constructive."[1]

The superintendent remembered loggers whose lives had been saved after great effort and danger to ship and crew, and whose thanks was a grudging, "Well, I guess I aint got no kick coming." The laconic language of a logger was like a wet blanket to churchmen whose approach was outgoing and ripe with sentiment. Some men dismissed the mission as "a bunch of damned parasites", complained the frustrated priest, and though they cheerfully dropped $25 in a poker game, baulked at contributing a cent to the work of the hospital ships.

At one point he deplored the poverty of soul that seemed to have succeeded the economic poverty of the Depression among the islanders. "They have become so self-sufficient that they seem utterly void of the sense of there being a life of the soul."[2] He had hoped that a blending of social and religious life would mean they would regard religion as something inextricably woven into their daily life, but their only interest, he felt in moments of despair, was in weekend dances and the "curse of strong drink." The lack of applicants for ship's chaplains and the short periods of service of those who answered the call perturbed him too. Unlike the Fundamentalists, he said, Anglican graduates seemed to want comfortable jobs in well-established parishes.[3]

But he would remember the warm welcome the ships were given in many lonely little coves, the joy that services on board or on the beaches gave to believers so far from city churches, and the thankful letters that dotted the pages of *The Log* from injured loggers saved by the quick action of the ships. The personal sympathy and support of the chaplains on these hospital trips meant much to the patients, and Greene even recalled a seasick bride clinging to his hand as she lay moaning on the ship's bunk throughout a rough trip. Greene had offered to ferry bride and groom on the first lap of their honeymoon after performing the wedding ceremony, but the bride felt her last hour had come as the ship plunged and rolled, and only the chaplain could comfort her.

Moments of disenchantment were inevitable as the dedicated chaplains encountered blocks of resistance among skeptics and holders of other faiths, and their persistence in offering aid to all is the more commendable when the difficulties and discouragements are realized. It is understandable that some clergymen preferred a parish church with faithful followers. Still, many sympathizers encouraged the chaplains and worked for them. Volunteers abounded, stepping in to help out temporarily during emergencies. Alan Greene visited Redrooffs (its early misspelling deliberately retained by residents) on days he could spare from his rounds. Here on the Sechelt peninsula, he and his son Alan were building the home that Greene and his wife planned to occupy after his retirement, and the arrival of the *John Antle* at the wharf at Redrooffs always brought out a flock of friends.

On one occasion Alan and his brother Heber were aboard, looking like twins, both short, stocky, and spectacled, each with a curly mop of white hair and a cheerful grin. Chris Dalton of West Vancouver and Redrooffs remembers his children running to catch the line as it was tossed to them across the water. They hauled lustily, and ended up with the whole of the line coiled at their feet. The brothers, famous for disorganization, had forgotten to attach the other end to the *John Antle*, which drifted slowly and inexorably away from the wharf.

Three generations of Daltons knew and loved the missionaries. Chris Dalton's father substituted for a time on the *John*

Antle as amateur engineer, and entertained his grandchildren with stories of his adventures aboard her. Two of the grandchildren were baptized by Greene in the tiny Church of His Presence that he had built at Redrooffs. "The only time our little boys scrubbed their faces and hands of their own accord was when Alan Greene's boat docked and they knew a service would be held on the beach. In these sermons, Alan directed many of the stories at the children; he was a marvellous raconteur," says Mrs. Dalton.[4]

The *John Antle* took over the Kingcome area while the *Gwa-yee* was off for repairs. At Gilford Island the Indians sat about on the grass while Alan Greene baptized babies at the portable altar and played hymns on the portable organ. In the evening he followed the practice of Rollo Boas, playing records over a loud-speaker from the roof of the ship's cabin.

The *John Antle* hit a rock off Lasqueti Island in 1947 and was taken to Vancouver for repairs to her stern. Coming back with her, Greene rescued off Point Atkinson a fisherman whose boat was rolling about in the slop with a broken crank shaft and towed him to shelter in Caulfield Cove. Back at Pender Harbour he was commandeered to be Master of Ceremonies at the crowning of the May Queen. Races followed, and Greene came in second in the 55-to-60 years event, winning himself 10¢. He still retained energy enough to last through the dance in the evening. The stamina of the Greene brothers was phenomenal.

2

Rollo Boas was another who voiced discouragement at times in *The Log*. He wrote that people depended on the mission for their doctor, dentist and nurse but showed little interest in the church services. Yet he too rejoiced in a faithful few, and cited a Sunday school held at Redonda Bay where 12 children met regularly at each other's homes for Bible instruction. He deprecated the educational system on the up-coast islands that closed down a school if the number of children registered was less than the required quota. There was no school at Stuart Island that year, and Boas helped the children with geometry problems when he called there in the *Rendezvous*.

Quick thinking and ingenuity were requisites for a coast missionary. Boas had just returned to Whaletown in the *Rendezvous* after taking Manson's Landing schoolchildren for a picnic, when he received a phone call from 90-year-old pioneer Ned Breeze who complained of great pain. The chaplain got the summer cruiser M.V. *Victor R* to stand by, and her crew helped him get old Mr. Breeze aboard the *Rendezvous* by means of a rope sling on the stretcher. He used the same method during the winter months to hoist a woman with a broken ankle over snow-covered rocks down to the sea and on to the ship.

The advanced age of most of the Columbia Coast Mission boats, and the rough waters they were forced to combat in the northern area may explain the prevalence of accidents at sea, though none were serious or involved loss of life. The *Columbia* hit ten-foot-high waves off Sointula in 1951, and those in the cabin suffered a salt-water showerbath. She could make only four miles an hour during the storm.

The *Rendezvous* with Rollo Boas encountered rough weather when taking Dr. Depew and several patients to the Campbell River Hospital. Once out of the harbour the ship twisted and turned as she rode the waves coming up behind her. The superstructure of the *Rendezvous* always caught the wind, and she rocked badly in a storm. On this occasion, waves broke over the cabin roof and surged under doors on to the cabin floor. Shelter was sought in Heriot Bay and the journey to Quathiaski made overland. At Quathiaski the patients, ranging from a small boy to an old age pensioner, ended their rough journey by climbing over the decks of five boats tied side by side, then clambering up an iron ladder to the deck of the big seiner that took them across Discovery Passage to Campbell River.

Lay preacher Donald Maclean of Whaletown wrote that a point of land just outside Whaletown was known locally as

"Thank God Point" because Boas, if he reached it safely in rough weather, always uttered a fervent "Thank you, God, for a safe trip home."

In 1953 the *Rendezvous* was navigating Surge Narrows rapids in a heavy flood tide when the engine suddenly died due to water in the fuel line. The ship was swept towards a huge rock in the centre of Beazley Pass; she bumped against it and passed, then the whirlpools caught her and she began to turn about in circles. Settler Walter Redford saw her spinning about from his ranch on Read Island and rowed out to her. He managed to catch her rope and towed her to the float by Tipton's store on Read.

The little 24-foot *Gwa-yee* at Kingcome had her troubles with stormy weather too. She headed out for Turnour Island where Ernest Christmas planned to give a service at New Vancouver village and was caught in a severe storm that blew up suddenly. At the float by the Indian reserve the missionary and his wife stayed aboard guarding the safety of the boat as the waves tossed and battered her about. For 36 hours neither Christmas nor his wife dared to undress or pause to sleep. Once the worst was over they gamely continued their services at Turnour and Gilford Islands between storms, thankful for a recently installed new engine. The *Gwa-yee* was really too small to face such weather, however, and three years later she was sold and the *Veracity*, a sailing yacht of 37 feet, was bought by the missionary. This ship was to be his own property although the Columbia Coast Mission agreed to pay operating expenses.

The 36-foot *John Antle* distinguished herself by pulling a small freighter five times her own size off a sandbar at Indian Point and into deep water, but Alan Greene on the same third *John Antle* had several experiences with sudden storms in 1950 that kept him hopping. When he went ashore for services he used to leave his cook, Stewart Holman, in charge of the ship, with instructions to blow the whistle if any trouble arose. One day he anchored the *John Antle* in Anderson Bay and reminded Holman to sound the ship's whistle if a storm arose as was expected. He had just begun a christening ceremony when the whistle sounded. The gale had struck! Greene hurried through the baptism in record time and got someone to run him out in a launch. The ship was nearly ashore, but the cook had managed to get the engine running and they raised the anchor and sped to the shelter of a little island, "narrowly missing a nasty reef."

Another time, Greene was just finishing a communion service on Merry Island when wheee! the whistle sounded and he looked out to see the *John Antle* running round and round in circles in the lee of the point. Once again the service came to an abrupt end and the chaplain was rushed out to the ship in the lighthouse tender. He found an offshore swell had dragged her moorings and anchor into deep water and she was drifting out to sea. Holman, being no seaman, had done the best he could to hold her back by circling near the lighthouse. The gale struck almost at once, and they fled from it into Smuggler Cove to wait out the storm.

3

Lighthouses were visited regularly by the mission ships, and patients were sometimes transferred to hospital, often a difficult task in stormy weather. Tiny Pine Island lies opposite the north end of Vancouver Island, surrounded by the stormy waters of Queen Charlotte Sound; often no landings can be made for months at a time. Percy Pike and his wife were the lightkeepers for many years and relieved the monotony of their isolation by harbouring a variety of wild life. Deer and rabbits were brought to the island and tamed for pets. There was only one possible landing place, a little cleft in the rocks behind the lighthouse, and here the Pikes had rigged up a cable running from a small power house down to the rocks. Their lifeboat was lowered to the cleft by means of a wire cable and pulley and, weather permitting, proceeded over the rolling swells to the *Columbia*.

Since the mission ship's lifeboat had no apparatus to attach it to the cable, contact with the ship was always made by means of the Pikes' boat. On one occasion a high wind came up while the lightkeepers were on board the *Columbia* for medical treatment and only experience and ingenuity in seamanship got their boat back to the cleft after a long hard fight through the great waves. The final landing on slippery rocks beside the cable was extremely tricky and had to be made in the brief moment between incoming swells.

Alan Greene was called to Merry Island lighthouse to take the keeper's wife, Mrs. Franklin, to hospital. They were forced to wait for good weather before attempting this awkward task. The lighthouse had a concrete runway from boathouse to sea, on which a small railway and trolley were set up to launch their tender. Mrs. Franklin was carried to the boathouse, then stretcher and all were laid in the lifeboat and sent down the incline, with the boat snubbed continually to keep it from running away.

Another lighthouse adventure involved Alan Greene and Ballenas light station. He was heading there in the *John Antle* III to give Christmas communion to Fred Bennett and his wife who were relief keepers. He found Fred at the lighthouse, but Mrs. Bennett had gone to their home on Gerald Island, leaving word for Fred to pick up their mail. Greene ran him to the mainland for the mail, then to Gerald Island to pick up Mrs. Bennett and a few things she wanted taken to the lighthouse.

The few things turned out to be five goats, 14 hens, two bantams, four ducks, two goldfish, a dog and a cat, all of which had to be herded on to a huge skiff and towed to the new home. Fortunately, Frank Ball of the *John Antle* crew was an ex-cowpuncher and he managed to round up these passengers calmly and competently. The two adult goats were wrestled into a crate and the kids hogtied in the bottom of the skiff. The hysterical hens were captured and thrust into a sack, the more philosophical ducks neatly boxed. The little banties lay quietly in a shopping bag, while the chaplain did his bit by carrying on the goldfish bowl. It was late when all were unloaded at the lighthouse, and the Christmas communion services had to be skipped that year.

4

The *Columbia* had a sad trip early in 1948 when an emergency call came from Seymour Inlet to pick up a young woman dying of tuberculosis. The *Columbia* braved a very high tide in the narrows to get to her quickly and was caught suddenly in a whirlpool and spun about in a complete circle that carried her perilously close to the cliffs. Captain MacDonald managed to get control before they crashed and the patient and her mother were brought aboard and taken to Alert Bay. Then chaplain Heber Greene realized that, just a year before, he had travelled 100 miles down the coast on the *Columbia* to officiate at the happy occasion of the young woman's wedding.

On March 4, 1948, the *Columbia* ran on to the tip of an uncharted rock in Warner Bay, Seymour Inlet. She was stranded there for several days. "Every creak and groan goes through my heart like a knife," Captain MacDonald told his wife as he waited for the damage to be assessed. The Straits Salvage and Towing Company refloated the ship and towed her 240 miles to Vancouver, where her hull was found to be damaged below the water line. She was off duty for a month. Captain MacDonald took over the *Columbia*'s territory with the *John Antle* for that month. Alan Greene was staying at Pender Harbour as the hospital was without a permanent secretary for a time. When the *John Antle* returned to Pender Harbour he made a few short cruises in her, with his 18-year-old daughter, Catherine, as crew.

At the time of the *Columbia*'s accident, Heber Greene had been on Hardwicke Island, setting out from there on tours of visits in the gas-boats of the Murphys and the Bendicksons. Both these families had numerous small children and there were always baptisms to perform as each generation came along. Heber visited 15 families on Hardwicke and at one time reckoned he had baptized about 15 Bendickson grandchildren and 13 Edwards grandchildren. Though logging camps on the whole were barren soil for religious conversion, the Bendickson logging company of father and sons was typical of many logging families who were sympathetic to the mission.

A number of figures prominent in the Columbia Coast Mission's history passed from the scene in the early 1950s. John Antle had died in 1949. The next year on August 14 the Reverend Canon Fred Comley died after long service as missionary and member of the mission board. Harold Auchinleck, long-time cook for the *Columbia*, who had brought happiness to hundreds of children in his role as the ship's Santa Claus and movie projectionist, died of a heart attack on May 13, 1950, and was buried at sea. Just before his death he had been appointed caretaker of a clubhouse for the elderly tenants of the mission's retirement homes (the Aged Folks' Guest Houses) near St. Mary's Hospital. These low-rental cottages were provided for those unable to cope in their old age with the rugged life of the north. In 1951 Dr. Nasmyth died of a heart attack on board the *Columbia* and his ashes were scattered in the sea from the ship by Heber Greene. Dr. John MacDonnell was a temporary replacement for Dr. Nasmyth on the *Columbia*.

Heber Greene was made Honourary Canon of Christ Church Cathedral in 1951, the same year that Alan Greene was made Honourary Canon of British Columbia, the Senior Priest of the B.C. Diocese.

In this year the Church of the Good Shepherd was built on Lasqueti Island on a site overlooking False Bay. Charles Williams and Compton Domvile of the Lasqueti Land Company donated the site to the mission, believing a church and community hall were urgently needed on the island. Bishop Gower dedicated the church on September 27, 1952, and services were held monthly by the chaplain of the *John Antle*.

The mission had administered St. Mary's Hospital at Pender Harbour from 1936 to 1953, but in 1953, due to a shortage of doctors and lack of finances, turned the hospital over to a local board. This ended hospital administration for the mission, although the ambulance boats continued their work and the *Columbia* maintained its floating hospital.

5

In 1953 the *Columbia* made a slow journey from Prince Rupert to Vancouver, towing the 12-year-old *Western Hope* to the Vancouver Shipyards to be overhauled and used as a Columbia Coast Mission ship, the fourth *John Antle*. She had been a mission boat in the Queen Charlotte Islands and was a gift to the Columbia Coast Mission from the Diocese of Caledonia. An earlier *Western Hope* had been wrecked in 1938 on Rose Spit in the Queen Charlottes. Her replacement was built in 1940 in Edward Wahl's Shipyard in Prince Rupert and was 44 feet long with an 11-foot beam. The Caledonia diocese had found her too expensive to run during the war years and she was kept idle until 1947 when she was towed from Masset to Prince Rupert and rebuilt; six years later she was presented to Alan Greene's fleet.

For her new assignment she was completely redesigned and fitted with a 165-h.p. gas engine, radio-telephone and modern equipment. Business firms and members of the Anglican Church contributed much of the cost of the fittings, while her compass and radio-telephone were memorial gifts. Alan Greene had raised $11,000 towards the cost and the Missionary Society of the Church of England in Canada gave $5,000, leaving only $2,000 outstanding.

Bishop Godfrey Gower, vice-president of the mission board, dedicated the ship on June 27, 1953 at the Vancouver Tugboat Company's wharf, Harold Jones having given permission for the ship to use his company's wharf. Ernest Antle, son of founder John Antle, was on the forward deck with his wife during the ceremony for the fourth ship to bear his father's name. The third *John Antle* was held in reserve, to be renamed if needed.

An interesting bit of equipment on the new vessel was the ship's bell which had formerly graced the pilothouse of the first *Columbia* in 1905. Some time after the *Columbia* had been dismantled, the Reverend Rollo Boas discovered it at Bliss Landing at the home of Mr. Wedig who had hung it outside his door as a dinner gong. He donated it to Boas who presented it in turn to the mission.

During the winter the new *John Antle* was taken on a run to Kingcome. The weather was bitterly cold and the crew were wearing up to five layers of clothing. The ship's whistle froze and could only emit "sounds like the last gasp of an asthmatic." The window wipers froze too, and a window had to be kept open to the icy blast so the skipper could see ahead. They reached Kingcome to find the river frozen over, and they had to slash the ice to get up. The Indians had cleared a trail to the mission house, and supplies were carried in on sleighs and by pack sack.

To their distress, after this painful journey they found that most of the Indians had turned from Anglicanism to the gospel according to Oral Roberts, the American evangelist. This was a blow, as they had found on a recent trip to Alert Bay that the Pentecostals had won over a good many converts. Missionaries of many religious persuasions were visiting up and down the coast at this time, in areas formerly assumed to be Anglican territory, and the mission recognized an urgent need for more priests and teachers.

At Kingcome, Ernest Christmas and his wife were working hard to remodel their new ship, the *Veracity*. They were felling trees for masts, and also planned to lay new flooring in her as well as making other alterations. A tremendous storm uprooted many trees, one of which fell across the deck of the *Veracity*, but luckily did her no great damage. A big problem was the task of supplying sufficient wood for the mission stoves during the long cold spell. Wood had to be towed by skiff, then sawed and carried to the woodshed. One large tree that they had secured to the bank, and which would have provided enough fuel for the winter, was swept away by a freshet and lost. Much firewood was needed, as three stoves were kept going when dignitaries paid their frequent visits to the mission house. On one occasion a stack they had hoped would be their winter's supply vanished during the visit of a large number of guests.

Another catastrophe occurred when the weight of a heavy snowfall caused the roof of the old mission house to cave in. Christmas patched up the roof after much strenuous labour, hampered by the deep snow, and using lumber largely salvaged from the wreck. He and his wife left Kingcome in the fall of 1954 for Pender Harbour, where they planned to help Alan Greene with Sunday services and to care for the guest houses for pensioners run there by the mission. This would leave Alan Greene with more time to travel on the new *John Antle*.

The *Veracity* received a rough send-off as she left Kingcome. She detoured to pay calls at the Indian villages before heading south. Thirty minutes after her start, her engines failed and she was towed by a fishboat to Simoom to have coil trouble corrected. Starting off once more, she hit high winds and had to lie awhile in Burial Cove. A fast run got her to better shelter in Port Hardy, but the edges of a Pacific typhoon struck the area. Four of the eight mooring ropes on the *Veracity* broke, and once again Ernest and Mrs. Christmas were up all night keeping their ship from smashing on the float or breaking loose from it. When at last the wind slackened, they headed on down to Pender Harbour.

Credit is due the elderly doctors who came out of retirement to fill temporarily the succession of vacancies on the *Columbia*. Dr. E. Mountjoy Pearse was in his 80s during his time on the ship, and Dr. F.O. Gilbert who replaced him was 79, a graduate in medicine of Toronto's class of 1902.

In 1954 Rollo Boas retired from service on the *Rendezvous*, and left in June for southern California to take a course in counselling. He and his family had enjoyed their ten years on beautiful little Cortes Island. Before leaving, he bought property there, and came up whenever possible to work on the house to which he eventually retired. When it burned down, he bought the mission property at Whaletown in 1969. The clinic had closed shortly before this date, and Boas adapted it for his family home, where he still resides.

6

Romance came to the little old *Rendezvous* in 1954 when she carried the new young chaplain and his bride on their honeymoon. Joe Titus, born on Grand Manan Island, New

Brunswick, had worked as a student missionary for the Columbia Coast Mission and expressed a hope at the time that he could be employed permanently on the boats as soon as he graduated from Wycliffe College. He had already earned his B.A. at the University of New Brunswick. After graduation, he planned to marry Joan McAvity, who would graduate in nursing the same year. The couple was considered an ideal replacement for Rollo Boas and his wife, and Titus was appointed in 1954 after ordination by Bishop Godfrey Gower. He took over the 30-year-old *Rendezvous* in July, was married in August, and the young couple set forth at once on their honeymoon.

Titus was deluged with advice on how and when to run the rapids. Five persons told him five different ways to navigate them, all different from the advice given him by Rollo Boas. He decided to follow the instructions of his predecessor who had learned through painful experience, and these proved to be right. That first year, Joan travelled with her husband on the *Rendezvous* tours. Like those before them who were unfamiliar with the British Columbia coast, Titus and his bride found everything novel and surprising, but they managed to cope, buoyed with the energy and enthusiasm of youth. Titus himself was a bit of a novelty to some of the coastal workers. He was tying up the boat at a wharf one hot summer day, wearing shorts along with his black shirt and dog collar, when a woman climbed out of a fishboat moored beside the *Rendezvous*. "My God!" she exclaimed, "I've got to get a picture of this!"

The variety of places in which he held his services intrigued him. A different setting offered itself at every stop: front rooms of homes, logging camp recreation rooms, bunkhouses, cookhouses, schoolrooms, his ship's cabin or the interior of some little country church. One thing was missing: a portable organ, by now an essential bit of equipment on the mission boats. Alan Greene sent out a request for one, but told him it would have to be larger and heavier than his own organ, the 32-pound "Little Jimmy", as the makers of Jimmy (Bilhorn of Chicago) were no longer in business.

Greene hoped that Titus could learn to play; it was

dangerous to employ volunteers as it was difficult to dispense with the services of unsatisfactory musicians once they were in charge. He recalled one very deaf old man who volunteered as organist. He would start off in one key and be moved to change to another. Then he would look up and strain to hear which key the congregation was following. Greene said he had to duck down behind the pulpit to keep his dignity and not be seen shaking with laughter as the singers leapt frantically from key to key.

Organists had their dilemmas too, especially with Little Jimmy which was too light to be stable. Greene brought the *John Antle* IV to a Christmas concert on Nelson Island, where Mrs. Harry Thomas volunteered to supply the music. Unfortunately, the floor of the hall was slippery from the wax applied preparatory to a dance, and as the player pressed the keys, Little Jimmy slid along in a steady glide, Mrs. Thomas hitching her stool to keep up, until a solid wall was reached and the chase ended.

The organ for Titus arrived that year and was named "Cecilia" after the Patron Saint of Music. She had been given to the *Rendezvous* as a memorial to W.P. Egerton, secretary and treasurer for the mission from 1935 until his death in 1952.

Titus was told that he would have to commit three errors to undergo a proper initiation to the west coast: running out of gas; going aground; and tying his boat fast without slack on an ebb tide. The first two happened that very summer. He ran out of gas in July, but fortunately was carrying a spare barrel. In August he was nosing the *Rendezvous* through a south-easter from Blind Creek to Savary Island when she suddenly stopped with a bump off Hernando Island and listed to port into the oncoming sea. It was nearly high tide, and the rock she had hit and run up on was hidden by the waves.

Luckily for the shipwrecked couple, the MV *Gulf Wing* came by shortly afterwards. She was a redesigned Fairmile corvette running a passenger and express service in competition with the Union Steamships on a route including Pender Harbour and points north. To the great entertainment of her passengers, who were busily photographing the proceedings,

the *Gulf Wing* attached lines and pulled the *Rendezvous* free.
The old boat gave a big list to one side as she came off the rock
and for a moment the missionary and his bride envisioned a
watery grave, but she righted herself and they got her safely to
Lund, where damage was found to be slight.

It was an eventful summer. The *Rendezvous* was anchored
in Cortes Bay near George Griffin's home one evening while
the chaplain and his wife went ashore to hold a service and
social hour. During the service, wind and rain began to shake
the windows and Titus realized a southeaster storm was
starting up. One of the men went out to see if the boat was
still in deep enough water and came back to say all was well.
After the movie and social hour, Titus slipped away to check
for himself and found the *Rendezvous* lying high and dry.
There was a rush to prop her up and pump out the water. It
was 1:30 a.m. before they finally floated her. Checking damages, they found the transmitter had been ruined by the salt
water; otherwise the sturdy boat had survived another batter-
ing by the waves, and Titus had now completed his three-
error initiation.

One dramatic incident after another marked the five-year stint
of the Reverend Joseph Titus. He had been warned, possibly
by someone with tongue in cheek, that the Indians were apt to
shoot at unwelcome visitors. He was approaching an Indian's
house on Stuart Island somewhat nervously when the man ran
out of the house with a shotgun and began firing. Titus
ducked behind a tree as bullets whistled about. When the
ammunition was exhausted, he emerged apprehensively and
the Indian, shaking his head in frustration, explained, "Those
darn goats just won't stay on their own side of the hill."

The *Rendezvous* was at Stuart Island on May 1, 1955, when
it suddenly became apparent that Joan was about to present
her husband with their first child. They caught a plane for
Campbell River, beating the stork by ten minutes. Stephen
was the first of three sons born to the couple during their five
years at Whaletown.

The third *John Antle* had been tied up since the launching
of her successor, with the idea of using her in emergencies.

Now in 1955 it was decided to rename her the *Laverock II*, after John Antle's little 14-foot dinghy that had braved the Yaculta Rapids in 1904. She would go to the clergyman skipper at Whaletown as a replacement for the *Rendezvous*.

Adventures continued with the *Laverock II*. Titus and his wife were on their way back from Campbell River after returning the dentist who had come for his monthly day at the clinic. They were bucking a stiff wind and heavy sea and were ten minutes from Whaletown when their engine stalled. Air had got into the fuel line, and Titus was unable to get the boat started. The heavy anchor was dropped, but the *Laverock II* continued to drift slowly towards the shore, forced in by wind and waves. The *Rendezvous* was tied up at the Whaletown wharf, with U.B.C. student helper Tom Anthony[5] aboard her, and Joan Titus suggested she could row ashore and get help from him while Joe stayed with the *Laverock II* to watch how the anchor was holding. The dinghy was lowered and Joan started off. Rowing was difficult in the choppy sea, and the boat began to leak. Soon the water was over her shoes. She stood up, dived over the side and began to swim through the waves towards the distant shore.

Now and again she trod water and shouted for help. Eventually Tom Anthony heard the cries, cast off and started out in the *Rendezvous*. He came on the swamped dinghy but saw no sign of Joan. Fearing the worst, he was about to start a search when he saw lights blinking on the shore and went back to find that Joan had made it safely to the beach. Frank Tooker and Tom went out in Tooker's boat, hauled up the anchor of the *Laverock II* and towed her to port.

The second Titus baby was born without benefit of doctor or nurse. Joan was alone at Whaletown as Joe had started off for Campbell River. Not long afterwards, a neighbour called at the vicarage with the gift of a cake and found the young mother in bed with a new baby boy just five hours old. Joe got to Campbell River and was met with the news that he had a second son. Gilean Douglas, Cortes Island author, and Mrs. Alan Greene came to the rescue and cooked meals for the clergyman and doctor who hurried to Whaletown and found mother and child doing well.

Dedicating fourth *John Antle,* 1953, at Coal Harbour, Vancouver
  (*Courtesy C.G. Tuck*)

The *Rendezvous* on the rocks, Coulter Bay, 1953. (*Courtesy Rev. J. Titus*)

Rev. and Mrs. J. Titus, c. 1955. (Courtesy C.G. Tuck)

The *Rendezvous* being pulled off rocks near Hernando Island by *Gulf Wing*, 1954. (Courtesy Rev. J. Titus)

The *Columbia*, *John Antle* and *Rendezvous*. (Courtesy Ralph A. Smith)

The third *Columbia* in Turnbull Cove, McKenzie Sound. Mt. Stephens in background. (*Photo by W.E. Nicholson*)

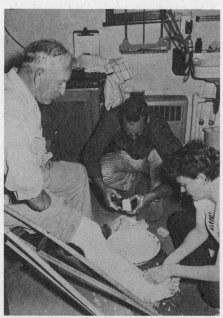

Dr. Mary Woods applying plaster cast aboard *Columbia*, 1957. (*Courtesy C.G. Tuck*)

Rev. Alan Greene playing Santa Claus, B.C. Forest Products camp, Jervis Inlet. (*Courtesy C.G. Tuck*)

Rev. Alan Greene christening babies at Gwyasdoms, Gilford Island. (*Courtesy Alan F. Greene*)

Canon and Mrs. Alan Greene. (*Courtesy Alan F. Greene*)

Canons Alan and Heber Greene.
(*Courtesy Vancouver School
of Theology*)

The *Laverock II*, formerly third *John Antle*, c. 1956. (*Courtesy Alan F. Greene*)

The fifth *John Antle*, 1957. (*Courtesy Vancouver School of Theology*)

.The fifth *John Antle*. (*Courtesy Rev. Trefor Williams*)

The *Alan Greene* being towed up Kingcome Inlet,
c. 1960. (*Courtesy Rev. Eric Powell*)

The *Che-kwa-la,* Kingcome Inlet, c. 1965. (*From* The Log)

Bowl, compass and "Little Jimmy" the organ. (*Courtesy Alan F. Greene*)

A chaplain's work is never done. Rev. Trefor Williams does his laundry, Knight Inlet. (*Courtesy Rev. Trefor Williams*)

Rev. Heber Greene and Rev. Eric Powell baptizing babies at King-come, c. 1960. (*Courtesy Rev. Eric Powell*)

Rev. Trefor Williams and Archdeacon P. Ellis holding Sunday school class on board the *John Antle,* c. 1962. (*Courtesy Rev. Trefor Williams*)

Archbishop Godfrey Gower, Canon (later Bishop) Hywel Jones,
Rev. Ivan Futter at dedication service on *Columbia IV,* 1968.
(*From* The Log)

Columbia IV at Guilford wharf. (*Photo by Gordon Sedawie*)

Throughout all these excitements, the usual work of the area was carried on by Titus: vacation schools, sermons, baptisms, weddings, summer picnics and Christmas parties. When least expected, dignitaries such as Bishop Gower or Dean Beattie would arrive to visit the boat or the manse, usually in the midst of a housecleaning or when the decks were being swabbed down, and young Mrs. Titus would undergo the embarrassment of all housewives when caught unprepared.

Missionaries coping with primitive living conditions at home and rough weather at sea were unhappy at times with city members of their board who decided their fate, often with no knowledge of the area and its problems. Most of these were poor sailors and had no desire to venture into stormy waters. Alan Greene once had Bishop Sexton aboard on a very rough trip around Cape Mudge. The bishop was violently ill in a basin provided by Greene. This little basin was known to the crew as the catholic basin as its use was all-inclusive: for washing hands, faces and dishes, peeling potatoes and rinsing out underwear. Greene proclaimed that henceforth the utensil would be known as The Bishop's Basin. The bishop was not amused. He made it clear that henceforth he would travel in nothing smaller than one of Her Majesty's ships.

His scheduled visit to Alert Bay was duly arranged with the navy. At the time, the Reverend Titus and his wife were on Cormorant Island. When delivering freight to Eric Powell at Kingcome, they had had an engine breakdown and were towed to the machine shop in Alert Bay for replacement of a broken part. While waiting, they walked down to the wharf, deserted at that hour, and watched as a naval vessel approached and docked. Off came Bishop Sexton, accompanied by a naval officer bedecked with medals and wearing a shining sword. A large car drove up, followed by a tiny Isetta. To the amusement of the young Titus couple, the naval officer and his sword were whisked away in the large car, while the tall bishop folded himself with great difficulty into the midget car, a three-wheeler without doors, whose whole front had to be opened up to take in the passengers.

It was the Bishop of the Diocese of Columbia, covering Vancouver Island and adjacent islands, whose part it was to inspect these areas, but Godfrey Gower, Bishop of New Westminster and vice president of the mission board, whose diocese was the mainland, was a more able seaman and did most of the travelling. He made Kingcome on the mainland his usual port of call, but stopped occasionally at the islands *en route*.

7

In the mid-1950s high school boys from the Shawnigan Lake School were working as substitute cook and deckhand on the fourth *John Antle*. Though their spirits were willing, their cooking skills were negligible and Alan Greene suffered. However, he was spending much of his time raising money for new ships to replace the 46-year-old *Columbia* and the fourth *John Antle*, the old *Western Hope*. He needed $125,000 and had raised $72,000 up to that time. He arranged one luncheon at which the B.C. Packers general manager was present and this netted him $40,000 in donations.

The *Laverock II* was offered to Bishop Watts of the Caledonia diocese for work in Masset Inlet in the Queen Charlotte Islands, as the Caledonia diocese had given the mission the *Western Hope* in 1953. The Reverend S.J. Leach of Masset Inlet Indian Mission and Mr. Walter Geryluk took over the *Laverock II* in October 1957. Before she left, the *Laverock II* travelled to Campbell River to carry the body of pioneer John Manson from the hospital to his home farm at Manson's Landing on Cortes for burial. Canon Greene was picked up at Lund and taken there to officiate at the funeral.

The fourth *John Antle* would replace the *Laverock II* as soon as the fifth *John Antle* was ready for service, and would be called the *Rendezvous*. The old *Rendezvous* was sold for $3000 in 1956. She was registered as *Tari Jacque* on January 10, 1956, by Edward C. Tooker of Whaletown and is still seen during the summers plying the coastal waters on Fisheries patrol.

The winter of 1955 was particularly cold and stormy, and extracts from the log of the *Columbia* give a picture of the hardships endured by the crew as they performed the very varied tasks expected of them. Throughout October there were strong gales: "southeast gale Oct 6 Clam Cove . . . strong SE Bull Harbour 10 stops." As they held a memorial service, baptism service, answered an emergency call and gave innoculations at Village Island it was "all SE gales" with fog and ice. At Port Elizabeth on October 27, the comment was simply "too rough." The doctor was listed as ill, but vaccinations continued during southeaster gales.

In November there were westerly gales around Stuart Point, strong gales every day, and two emergency calls during "snow and sleet." In December the *Columbia*'s log says they were at Pine Island, "too rough to come off." An odd entry states "10 dogs' tails bobbed." An emergency call to Minstrel Island was made in heavy snow and wind, there was a blizzard at Port Neville, and at Hardy Bay it was snowing and too rough to land. Later they got stuck in the mud trying to get into the bay.

In January at Garden Bay they took on a piano for Village Island and set off in sleet and a southeast gale. On January 25 they recorded the first fine day in months, but were right back into snow and ice every day after that as emergency calls kept coming in. "Too much ice" says the captain's log.

During that bitter winter, the *Columbia* was up Seymour Inlet when Captain George MacDonald fell on the icy deck and broke his hip. Dr. Molly Towell and the crew had great difficulty moving the injured man from the slippery deck to the hospital area. Two loggers at the camp they were visiting volunteered to run the ship south to Alert Bay, where the valiant captain who had served the mission so long and so well was put on a plane for Vancouver and St. Paul's Hospital. There, two plates and three steel pins were inserted in his hip, a comparatively new procedure.

Bob McCrea, the *Columbia*'s engineer who had been 12 years with the mission, acted as her captain on the next trip, and they carried on for a time with Masato Araki as engineer, Lew Toy as cook and the physician, Dr. Molly Towell, who continued with them for a short period before leaving for England. Heber Greene was still the *Columbia*'s priest.

The new *Columbia*, third vessel of four in the mission service to bear the name, was launched in 1956. Bishop Godfrey Gower performed the dedication service on October 13 and she was christened by Mrs. Gower. Captain MacDonald, on crutches after his accident, attended with Mrs. MacDonald. He was unable to return to work on a permanent basis after his operation, and retired.

The graceful *Columbia* II, after 46 years with the mission, was sold and became a charter yacht, first known as the *Wayward Lady* and later bought and renamed *Lady Valentine* by Eric Griffiths of White Rock. She was up for sale again in 1975 but was destroyed by fire while docked in Annacis Slough the following year, ending 66 years of steady service.

The third *Columbia* was about 65 feet overall, built at Star Shipyards in New Westminster. She was smaller than her predecessor and could be run with a crew of four, whereas five were needed to man the second *Columbia*. During 1958 there was a succession of crew replacements for her. There were four captains and three chaplains in the space of four months, while the rapid turnover of doctors continued.

8

Alan Greene's enthusiasm for his ships and the beauties of the Inside Passage was shared by Bishop Godfrey Gower (at present Archbishop, retired.)[6] Gower delighted to travel from one end of the passage to the other on the *Columbia* and the *John Antle*, dedicating ships, holding confirmation classes on board, and going by Indian canoe up the river to Kingcome to baptize babies (including the great grandchild of Ernest Halliday, the pioneer settler.)

The bishop was often asked to explain the fascination that Kingcome held for him. The journey north could be rough, the trip up the inlet and river might be made in driving rain, the destination was a small Indian village. But one visit to

Kingcome in fair weather was an enchantment that could compensate for many an ordeal. He holds dear the memory of an Easter sermon held in St. George's Church. At that time there was a window of clear glass behind the altar, and the bishop could see the snow-capped mountains framed in the window. Just as he reached a culminating point in the service, the sun rose from behind the mountains, flooding them with light. It was symbolic, to him, of the beauty and peace of this isolated valley. He felt also a deep rapport with the Kwakiutl natives and during his many visits developed lasting friendships. There is a picture of the bishop wearing a cherished button blanket that was among the gifts he received from them.

Archbishop Gower has a lively sense of humour. One of his stories concerns a baptismal service in St. George's Church at Kingcome. About a dozen Indian babies had been brought by their godparents to the portable font set up in front of the congregation. Alan Greene, assisting the bishop, chose a plump, placid baby for the first baptism, hoping it would set a calm precedent for the infants to follow. But the minute the holy water dampened its brow the baby uttered a yell of protest, and every infant promptly joined in with lusty shrieks, arms and legs waving violently as godparents struggled to hold them. In the midst of the uproar a little dog ran up the aisle and prepared to use the altar as a substitute fire hydrant. Priests and godparents leapt to drive off this small profaner. The congregation held its breath in horror for a moment, then burst into shouts of uncontrollable laughter. The babies were eventually baptized, but holy water had been scattered far and wide in the confusion.

Archbishop Gower recollects a trip on the *John Antle* with Greene, coming south through Johnstone Strait, Discovery Passage and the Strait of Georgia. Greene felt thoroughly at home on the coastal waters by now and liked to travel at full speed, steering by instinct. A fierce storm struck as they emerged from Johnstone Strait. It was pitch dark, the ship rolled and plunged, and at one point there was a jarring thud as they grazed a rock or deadhead. "Must have hit something," Greene said cheerfully, without slackening speed.

As the storm increased in fury, Greene announced that out of consideration for the less seasoned traveller he would cast anchor in a sheltered cove for the remainder of the night, and he turned into a bay on Lasqueti Island. He spread a sleeping bag on the pilot's table for himself and gave up his bunk to the bishop. The winds had changed and now blew directly into the bay, rolling the ship about so that Gower was unable to sleep, though with his long legs he was fitted into the bunk so tightly, head and feet wedged against the bulkheads, that he himself remained immobile. About two a.m. he fell asleep, only to be wakened almost at once by a resounding thump. Alan Greene had been tossed off the pilot's table by a sudden sideways lurch of the ship. Gower took great pleasure the next morning in chaffing the veteran skipper on his strange idea of a sheltered cove and on the shameful fact that Greene had fallen from his bed while Gower lay motionless throughout the night. Greene's reputation of enjoying the discomfiture of guests during rough voyages added much to the bishop's satisfaction.

On a serious note, the archbishop recalls a dark, stormy night that he spent on the *Columbia* when five separate emergency calls were answered. It was debatable whether or not the ship should venture out at all, but Captain MacDonald decided to go. He had always seemed to have a directional instinct that guided him through the dark without the aid of radar. He said he could sense or smell the islands. Before the night was over, the *Columbia* had taken to the hospital a small child blinded by a kettle of boiling water it had pulled from the stove onto its head, a man burned by an exploding pressure cooker, a settler with a bad sprain, a woman in labour, and a man who had fallen into a bush of the long-spiked devil's thorn and developed an infected knee. This last patient, incidentally, refused to pay for the treatment.

Heber Greene, the *Columbia*'s chaplain, was as active as ever during his final year before retirement in June 1958. His brother compared him to Sputnik, the Russian satellite launched in 1957, as he dashed about: ("There it is! Now where is it?") Sometimes he took planes from place to place ("Times are changing," he said.) He left tangible evidence of his work in the churches he built at Sayward and Port Hardy.

On one of his last trips, the *Columbia* took him 90 miles up Knight Inlet, after which he travelled by speedboat up the Klinaklini River to the D.O.T. Logging Company. At Camp Logco the black bears had become so tame they were allowed into the building and were fed by hand by the loggers. In the morning Heber saw a mother bear and cub playing in front of the verandah. An electric fence had been erected around the vegetable patch, the one place where the bears were not welcome.

This was the locale of Beth Day's book, *Grizzlies in their Back Yard*, and Jim and Laurette Stanton, about whom the book was written, came downriver and on board the *Columbia* to meet the crew. The Stantons had come from Seattle in 1919 to live in the British Columbia wilderness where Mr. Stanton acted as a guide for sportsmen. They still considered it a paradise after nearly 40 years among the grizzlies.

After this, diabetes and injuries sustained during his travels ashore impaired the health of Heber Greene, but the beloved canon was still in great demand by the settlers. His wanderings about the country had made him familiar with families throughout several generations, and those he served thought of him fondly as an integral part of their lives. The Reverend Futter in later years was preparing to conduct a wedding service when the parents of the bride told him, "You know, we've never been sure we were properly married, ourselves. Dear old Heber Greene had just reached the words 'Do you take ...' when he stopped short and began to reminisce about the time he had married our parents. Then he said 'I now pronounce you man and wife' and we hadn't the heart to tell him that a part of the vows had been omitted."

After Heber Greene's death in 1968, Archbishop Gower wrote in part in the *Anglican Synod Journal* of that date: "Amongst a variety of colourful personalities, whose names are household words, is that of Canon Heber Greene, who died on Friday, May 31st, aged 80 years... It was while spending a holiday in the Mission Ship that I first came to know him. I was taken by his gentleness and I admired his simplicity. He had that rare gift of interior discipline and was never far away in his thoughts from the presence of God. He was remarkably well read and was one of the few clergy who could read his daily New Testament lessons in Greek. The physical hardship of his work he took in his stride and never complained . . . We thank God for Heber Greene."

9

The fifth *John Antle,* last ship to bear the founder's name, was built by Star Shipyards in New Westminster in 1956 and launched on January 26, 1957. Alan Greene's daughter Catherine had sent a magnum of Atlantic sea water from Halifax for the christening, and this was mixed with water from the Pacific Ocean as symbolic of the sea by John Antle's Newfoundland birthplace and the waters of the western ocean where his mercy ships sailed for so many years. Mrs. Alan Greene christened the ship, giving the bottle a hefty swing that shattered it to bits, but forgetting in her excitement to pronounce the ship's name. Nevertheless, the *John Antle* stood up to her first trial trip when Greene took her out in a gale to test her. She kept well on her course, and a weekend guest on her, Captain Lawrence J. Goudy, R.N., said, "You have a well-found little ship, skipper."

Canon Greene agreed. This was his favourite ship, according to his son Alan, who says it was built to his father's specifications in just the way that he felt was best for a missionary ship. She was 46 feet overall length, with a 13-foot beam, fitted with a General Motors diesel engine and could reach a speed of ten knots. Her pilothouse equipment had been presented by Mr. Leo Chard in memory of his granddaughter Anne Birkett who was to have joined the summer staff of the mission but was drowned just before the date she was to commence work. The complete furnishings of the pilothouse and the ship's lifeboat were paid for by Anne's mother. The Community Chest of Victoria granted $1000 a year towards operating expenses of the *John Antle.* Canon Greene called the two ships the Jubilee ships, as just over 50 years had passed since the first *Columbia* was launched in 1905. In 1955 he had issued a special number of *The Log,* the Jubilee Issue, a pictorial history of the Columbia Coast Mission up to that date.

The second *Rendezvous,* formerly known as the fourth *John Antle* and before that as the *Western Hope,* was turned over to Joe Titus early in March 1957. She was a bigger boat than the *Laverock II* and had a wider turning circle. Practice was needed before Titus learned to dock her neatly. He had an interested and amused audience at Stuart Island the first time he took her there. The tide was going out fast as he made a series of circles unsuccessfully, each one a bit farther out along the float. By the time he got her in close enough to tie her up, the tide was out so far that the *Rendezvous* had to be docked at the very end of the long float. However, he made it in time to baptize Marie, the youngest daughter of the Brimacombes, owners of the first fishing resort on Stuart Island at Big Bay.

The little church that Rollo Boas built, St. Saviour's-by-the-Sea in Cortes Bay, was dedicated that year. Bishop Dean, Canon Heber Greene, the Reverend Tom Robinson and the Reverend Joseph Titus were all on hand, some arriving on the *Columbia* and some on the *John Antle.*

With the need for marine ambulances rapidly declining, there was a certain satisfaction in 1958 when the *Rendezvous* replaced an aircraft during an emergency pick up. She was called to transport an injured logger from Read Island during a southeaster storm. The seas were breaking into the small bay and the plane was unable to land in the surging swells. The *Rendezvous* with Joe Titus made it into the bay and tied up to another small vessel. The patient was placed on a stretcher, and helpers divided themselves, some to guide the stretcher, others to tend the spring lines, and still others to watch the fenders as the ships rolled about in the swell. The *Rendezvous* got back to Whaletown, where the plane was able to land and fly the patient on to Campbell River Hospital.

A third son was born to Joan and Joseph Titus on February 4, 1958. The chaplain's parents had come out from New Brunswick to spend that winter at the vicarage, and Titus had his father as helper on the *Rendezvous* during his tours of the islands, including the Christmas cruise. After four years with the mission, Titus, like most of the chaplains with families, was ready for shore life. In 1959 he was called to the Diocese of Fredericton, but was back in the west three years later as Naval Chaplain at Royal Roads, Esquimalt, and chaplain for the *Naden*. Still later he was called to parish work in Victoria.

10

Canon Alan Greene had realized his ambition to see replacements for his ships before his retirement. The *Columbia* and the *John Antle* were newly built, and the *Rendezvous* could face a few more years of winter storms. Now Greene turned his organizing ability to raising money for a ship for the Kingcome area. Eric Powell had served as a deckhand on the *Columbia* in 1951, worked in a Seymour Inlet logging camp and served as a student priest at Kingcome during several summers, but now as the Reverend Eric Powell, graduated from the University of British Columbia and the Anglican Theological College, he was free to give year-round service.

For 80 years the Anglican Church had been the recognized church for the Alert Bay and Kingcome areas, but with numerous other denominations moving in, it was essential to supply the young missionary with a ship so he could keep in touch with the Indian villages at Kingcome, Gilford Island, Village Island and New Vancouver on Turnour Island. It was expected that Powell would take young Indians as ship's helpers on his visits to the islands and the hope was that some of these would become Anglican missionaries to their people.

On November 14, 1959, the mission ship *Alan Greene* was

launched at Bissett's Boat Building Yards in North Vancouver on a dismal day of heavy snow and cold wind. Two years of canvassing by Canon Greene had raised money from many sources to cover the cost. Mrs. Ernest Christmas christened the ship and the *Alan Greene* sailed successfully down the ways. Robert Allan and his son who had shared in the design of the ship had come to watch the launching as she slipped into the water, her bow draped with a huge C.C.M. flag that Eric Powell had placed there. She was 35 feet overall with a ten-foot beam and was furnished with an 65-h.p. Perkins diesel engine.

Bishop Godfrey Gower dedicated the ship two weeks later, with Canon Alan Greene giving an address that told the history of the Kingcome Indian mission and the island villages. A new mission house to replace the building at Kingcome wrecked by heavy snowfall was in process of construction by Powell, materials supplied through the financial backing of the oldest missionary society in England, the New England Company. Powell left shortly after this for Kingcome in the *Alan Greene*, with a young Indian from Kingcome, Ernest Willie, sailing with him as guide and helper. Ernest Willie, as had been hoped, became in time an Anglican priest.

Powell proved his worth in Kingcome. He respected the traditions and culture of the Kwakiutl people and in return many of them accepted Powell's teachings as not incompatible with their own beliefs. Like all missionaries on the coast he had his days of frustration when he found his congregations in the villages swaying towards the teachings of the "fine weather" preachers, a name they gave to the exponents of various denominations who travelled up north only during the summer months. Sometimes when he returned to Kingcome after a discouraging visit to the island villages, he would be hailed by Vic Bota, a logger at a camp in Moor Bay at the head of the inlet. "Well, preacher, how's your trapline? Anybody poaching on it?" would come the shout, and Powell's laugh and ever-ready smile would show that his spirits had risen again, buoyed by that essential ingredient of survival, a good sense of humour.

There had been some doubt at first that Powell should be permitted to undertake the arduous work at Kingcome. While a student working for the Forestry Department he was the victim of a car accident. He was driving out of the woods to send a telegram of congratulation to his brother on the brother's wedding day when the car went out of control on a bridge and dropped 85 feet into a ravine. Despite his injuries, Powell walked 1½ miles to a farmhouse to get help for the other passengers. Partially paralysed for six years, he had a long fight to regain his health. However, his enthusiasm and his rapport with the Indians were deciding factors.

In 1961 Powell was transferred to Westview, a less taxing post. Though Ron Deane took over Kingcome, Powell flew frequently to the Indian village to conduct services. During this period, Kingcome was visited by the American author, Margaret Craven. She came to gather material for a novel on the village, flying to Powell River, then travelling to Kingcome on the *John Antle*. She was wearing a tight wool skirt for the trip and it was a struggle for her to climb to the boat deck. She said she had been told that she would not be allowed on a missionary ship wearing slacks. She was reassured that informal nautical attire was permissible, and the *John Antle* stopped off in Simoom Sound at a floating store which sold her its last pair of slacks.

The author asked innumerable questions about the mission and about Indian stories and legends. Due to failing eyesight she took several years to complete her book, but the result was the popular novel, *I Heard the Owl Call My Name* (dedicated to Eric Powell), which was made into a film. It is interesting to read this charming, romanticized account and speculate about what is fiction and what is fact, and which of the characters are obviously based on real people that the author met. Many a reader wept over the death of the young priest in Craven's book, but Powell, his health recovered, is now the very active Director of Programs at the Anglican Synod in Vancouver, and a member of the mission board. He makes regular visits to Kingcome, and Indians often contact him for help and advice.

11

The *Rendezvous* was taken over by the Reverend Trefor Williams, a short, sandy-haired bundle of energy born in Beaumaris, North Wales. While he was still in college, Williams came across a Columbia Coast Mission booklet and was inspired to write to Canon Greene. Eventually he left his parish in the Diocese of Chester, England, and came out to Vancouver in February 1959, his family following later. Greene, who was to retire in December of that year, was on hand to meet the new chaplain. Williams arrived at ten a.m. and by 11 o'clock Greene had introduced him to Bishop Gower and Archdeacon Thompson, he had been licensed, had signed innumerable documents and was on board the *Columbia* meeting the crew. "Gosh! The C.C.M. sure works fast!" exclaimed Williams. The board was indeed eager to gather him to the fold. Optimistically they hoped that finally they had found an experienced sailor-chaplain with enough enthusiasm to stay permanently with the job.

Greene went with him on the *Columbia*, Captain W.E. Nicholson skippering, for a tour of the C.C.M. area. They started off when the forecast was for strong southeast gales. Williams had heard of Greene's reputation for taking land-lubber clergy to sea during bad weather and revelling in their discomfort, but he was able to disappoint the canon. Heavy weather held no terrors for him after his seafaring experience with the merchant service during the war and the years that he had sailed small craft along the English and Welsh coasts. He exhibited no signs of sea-sickness, but was exhausted at times when every evening, often after a hard day of work, Greene invariably demanded at least three games of chess.

Like Boas, and like Titus whom he visited on Cortes Island on this trip ("driving around the Island in a crazy truck which ran out of gas three times"), Williams was stymied by logging language. When he asked for an explanation of words such as choker, cat-skinner, whistle punk, donkey and dutchman he got answers involving half a dozen more unintelligible words.

On the new chaplain's first day on the *Rendezvous,* he left for Kingcome accompanied by Titus, and by Alan Greene who wished to see what progress Eric Powell was making with the building of his new mission house. They got up there without mishap, but on the return trip, after leaving Alert Bay their engine overheated, the usual southeaster storm started up and they began to drift towards a rocky shore in the gathering dusk. They called Alert Bay by radiophone asking for help, but only a tug was in port and it would be two hours before the slow vessel could reach them. Fortunately an American ship *en route* to Alaska passed by, saw their plight and came to their rescue. Titus and Williams struggled to pass a heavy tow line up to the great ship towering above them. They succeeded and the ship started off; then the tow parted and the job had to be done all over again. In the process the two vessels rolled together and the *Rendezvous* lost her taffrail. They got back to Alert Bay at midnight.

Returning to Whaletown, Williams helped Titus load luggage and took him to Vancouver, where Williams met his wife as she arrived from England with their son Stephen and a new son, Christopher, whom he saw for the first time.

Despite his years with the merchant marine, Trefor Williams discovered a trip around Cape Mudge in a storm could be a shattering experience. The *Rendezvous* dived and rolled so violently that all his papers, books and crockery landed in a heap on the deck. His deckhand, Andy Livingstone, was away at the time and Williams had to cook, wash dishes and decks, and get up in the night in the pouring rain to move the ship in case she went aground. He thought of his peaceful days in the Diocese of Chester when he had only to stroll from home to a waiting church and stationary organ. Here, he often packed the organ on his back as he climbed a hill to hold his service in a school or log cabin. But, he philosophized, "Not for ever by still waters would we idly rest and stay."[7]

The organ was a year-round problem. Like most of the priests who were expected to be jack-of-all-trades, Williams was no musician. He sent out an urgent request to mission headquarters to supply him with sheet music for hymns that could be played with two fingers.

There could be hazards even without storms. The *Rendez-vous* was tied up at Campbell River one Saturday night. Over 80 seiners, gill-netters and small boats filled the harbour, tied up five abeam. About 3:30 in the morning an Indian boat in the centre of the fleet started up its engine. Half an hour later there was a terrific explosion and the *Rendezvous* seemed to be picked up and thrown down again with violent force. The Indian fishboat was a mass of flames and there was utter confusion as all the boats struggled to get free. The *Rendezvous* got out stern first. The cause of the explosion, which killed the fisherman, was unknown.

12

Alan Greene's long service with the mission, dating from 1911, ended with his retirement on December 31, 1959. He was 70 years old. He had watched the progress of the Columbia Coast Mission as it grew from small beginnings to an active fleet servicing three hospitals, had seen the loss of the hospitals due to lack of funds, and the building of roads and airplane landing fields that were diminishing the need for hospital ships. Antle had broken the ground, showing the urgent need in the early 1900s for hospital and ambulance service. Greene had had the equally difficult task of proving the importance of satisfying the spiritual and social needs of the settlers through the work of a marine service, and in the field of spiritual and social care many denominations and organizations were canvassing for funds.

Alan Greene was an ideal public relations man, with the necessary stamina, ability to dramatize the mission's needs, and an amiable manner that forestalled resentment against his constant appeals. The homely humour that coloured his talks in churches, at wedding receptions and gatherings of settlers is still remembered with affection up and down the coast. At his last Christmas party and service at Lasqueti Island, the wife of logger Jack Holland said, "Maybe we don't all go to church, but what will we do without you for our weddings and christenings and parties? We've known you so long and you know us so well."[8]

Pender Harbour honoured him with a large gathering of well-wishers who presented him with a cheque for $950. He spent this, predictably, on a speedboat, and passed his happy years of retirement hurtling over the waters by Redrooffs on the Sechelt peninsula, where he had built a home.

With the canon went his beloved portable organ, Little Jimmy, that had been with him since his first days with the mission, on nearly 5000 voyages. Five new covers of plywood had been given the little instrument over the years. Countless memories, sad and happy, were evoked by Little Jimmy: memories of packing it through the bush to play hymns in logging bunkhouses; of hauling it up rocky cliffs to tiny schoolhouses on remote islands; of picking out the joyful notes of the wedding march for bride and groom in the cabins of a succession of mission ships; of setting it up on beaches of island reservations while Indian babies were baptized into the Anglican faith; of hymns sung on deck during burials at sea. It may be seen today, along with the compass and bowl from the *Columbia*, on exhibition at Vancouver's Maritime Museum.

Alan Greene died at 83 and his ashes were scattered over the waters of Welcome Pass. He was survived by his second wife Dorothy[9] and his five children. "We mourn the going of the last of the great sea-going priests," said the Reverend Eric Powell at the funeral in Sechelt on October 13, 1972. He spoke of Canon Greene as "a man of strong conviction, infinite humility, warm and compassionate." Bishop David Somerville conducted the memorial service in Vancouver's Christ Church Cathedral.

Conditions on the coast had altered considerably by the time Alan Greene retired in 1959. There were far fewer logging camps, and those in existence were run by large companies with sophisticated machinery requiring fewer men to operate. Small canneries had closed down, bought out by large companies to eliminate competition, or forced to close as the enormous fish runs of the early days became a thing of the past. These changes resulted in loggers, cannery workers and fishermen moving to new jobs in the cities. Roads opened up new lanes of travel and planes were rapidly superseding boats for emergency runs. In January 1959, the historic Union Steamship Company sold out, ending its 67 years of service.

For a decade, the spectre of plane service had haunted those who loved the boats and felt the service would collapse without them. Back in 1950, Alan Greene had foreseen the shifting to air travel and put in a plea for the ships. In his superintendent's report for that year he wrote: "You will always have to give thought to ships and their maintenance, as ships are the only means of keeping in touch with, and serving, the extraordinarily interesting people our Mission serves. The aeroplane has been suggested as a means of covering our patrols, but I am convinced that were we to resort to such, our clergy and lay-workers would lose that intimate touch that a little ship makes possible and inevitable, as she travels day and night into places very difficult for a plane to reach. The very fact that a small ship MUST find anchorage for a night in some tiny harbour, where people have settled, leads to hundreds of evenings spent by the ships' crew in the homes of the people."

In 1959 one of several survey committees was formed to study the feasibility of retaining the marine missionary work. Serving on the committee were Derek Lukin Johnston, Archdeacon A.E. Hendy, Mr. Vernon Kirkby, Cecil Fitzgerald (who sailed two days on the *Rendezvous* to assess the situation) and the Reverend Patrick Ellis, who was to succeed Greene as superintendent at the end of the year and who sailed three days on the *John Antle*. The Reverend Trefor Williams and the Reverend Eric Powell were also asked to comment. The consensus was that the only urgent need for medical work was in the territory of the *Columbia*. The new road to Lund could provide transport for emergency cases in the south, and only a residential priest was needed there. The *John Antle* and *Rendezvous* should work in the central area, visiting all denominations.

Cecil Fitzgerald wrote to Ellis recommending that priests spend more time in the field and less at their home base. Not yet won over to plane service, he pointed out that planes were speedy but could not land on rocky beaches or fly during fog.

That year in December, Quadra Island fisherman Lloyd Vaughn anchored his boat at the head of Bond Sound, a little inlet off Tribune Channel, about 20 miles south of Kingcome Inlet. During the night he was wakened by cries for help and saw an Indian rowing towards him in a small skiff. His boat, anchored nearby, was burning fiercely from stem to stern. Vaughn took him aboard and ran him to Buzzard's camp where he had seen the *Columbia* as he passed there that day. The Indian, Arthur Boundsound of Alert Bay, was treated on board the *Columbia* for his painful burns and taken the 40 miles to Alert Bay where the police met the ship, conveyed the patient to hospital and took his skiff into custody for safekeeping.

Chapter Six

The Last Years

I

The Reverend Patrick R. Ellis became the third superintendent of the mission at the start of 1960. Tall and personable, in his 40s, he was a serious, practical man in sharp contrast to the humorous, unsystematic Greene brothers. He had agreed to leave his large city parish of St. Paul's in Vancouver and serve for a maximum of five years with the mission, continuing the evaluation of the marine service. As administrator, he was given the title of Archdeacon of Quatsino. Ellis and his wife, the former Margaret Galloway, moved with their five children to Campbell River at the time of his appointment, and Campbell River became his headquarters.

Patrick Ellis, son of a minister in Hampshire, England, had come with his parents to Comox as a boy of 16. He studied accountancy and taught in a commercial school, then switched to theology. He graduated from the University of British Columbia and the Anglican College, spending several summers during his student days with Alan Greene on the first *Rendezvous*. After ordination he served two years in the Princeton area, two at St. George's in Vancouver and nine years at St. Paul's. He was with the air force in Canada and overseas from 1942 to 1946.

Ellis had little background as a seaman, apart from his deckhand work with the *Rendezvous*. His first interest in the sea seems to have been after his appointment as superintendent, when he acquired a 16-foot sailboat and enjoyed pleasure boating. Emotion thus played no part in his evaluation of the mission boat work.

Mainly it was his practicality as a former accountant that let him face squarely the fact that life in the area had changed radically since the beginning of the mission and resulted in his decision to modify the service accordingly. At this time the mission consisted of five priests, seven layworkers, three ships, six churches, a mission house and clinic and a head office. Maintaining these required $60,000 annually. Ellis implemented the recommendations of the Special Committee to retain the third *Columbia* and remove the fifth *John Antle* from her Pender Harbour base, keeping her along with the *Rendezvous* on the Cortes Island patrol in the central area from Cortes north.

In a letter to Bishop Gower, Ellis also recommended abolishing the office of superintendent, thereby saving the cost of running the headquarters office and paying a superintendent. A parish under the Columbia diocese with headquarters at Whaletown would suffice, the *John Antle* could be sold, the months spent in campaigning for funds for her upkeep eliminated, and with the money from her sale he suggested buying a Cessna 172 plane.

Archdeacon Ellis had asked John Antle's son, Ernest Antle, to estimate the cost of running a plane service to replace the ships. Ernest regularly covered the *Columbia*'s area by plane during logging work with his company, Antle Scaling and Grading Ltd. Unlike his father, Ernest found the seas boring. He believed the mission work could be accomplished more quickly and economically by plane, and worked out costs for a Supercub and a Cessna. He referred to the Reverend Carl Major of Battle Harbour Mission in Newfoundland who flew a Supercub, *Laverock II*, and wrote to Ellis, "I think that the air may produce dedicated men to a greater extent than the sea." He hammered his point home by quoting a line from

McGee's "High Flight": "Put out my hand, and touched the face of God."[1] Ellis was convinced, and was successful in placing Antle on the mission board, to present his arguments to the members and help to overcome any opposition.

Now the *Rendezvous* was run by two lay preachers, George Barber and Peter Price, and Trefor Williams took over the *John Antle,* both ships covering sections of the central area. The first task of Williams on the *John Antle* was to convey the body of Mr. Richard Symons of Evans Bay, Read Island, to the crematorium in Campbell River. As usual, a southeaster was blowing, and the coffin had to be lashed to the deck as the ship rounded Cape Mudge. Twenty-six persons crowded aboard the *John Antle* and several boats accompanied her as she headed out to sea and scattered the ashes from her deck into the waters of the passage.

On the *John Antle* during the months that followed, Williams experienced his first encounters with the fierce Bute winds and the wild Yaculta Rapids. In winter, turbulent waters swept his decks, leaving them sheeted with ice. He suggested to the Survey Committee the substitution of a speedboat for his work, being less costly and allowing him to get home quickly, but the idea was quashed. A speedboat could not run at night in those waters and service at all hours was the policy of the marine fleet. At the close of 1961, after three years with the mission, Williams opted for shore life and the mission was once again without a sailor chaplain for its small boats. Williams was called to the Campbell River diocese, and later to Victoria where he began a strenuous life in varied parish work, his home and office a picturesque old mission building, his sea days confined to cruising on his sailboat in calmer waters.

2

The second *Rendezvous* was sold in May 1961 to Great Northwest Charter Lines of North Vancouver who planned to run her for three months in the summer in Queen Charlotte

Sound. She was skippered by Captain George Barber and further enhanced her reputation as a mercy ship when she rescued six persons from the sinking fish-packer *Great Northern I* on June 20, 1962. The packer ran aground and broke up just after the *Rendezvous* took off her crew. Later the *Rendezvous* was sold to Rendezvous Dive Ventures Ltd. of Port Alberni.

Romance came again to the ships, this time the *Columbia*, when Captain W.E. Nicholson married Flying Officer Margaret Westover of Hawkins, Kent, on July 7, 1961, in St. George's Chapel, Alert Bay. The Reverend Eric Powell conducted the service for Captain Nicholson and his bride, who had met when the captain was on a holiday in England. The board had asked him to contact a woman there in connection with mission work and through her he was introduced to his future wife.

The *Columbia* was tied up in Victoria for a time in an effort to advertise the work of the mission to Victoria citizens. Various dignitaries visited her, including Lieutenant-Governor Pearkes, with resultant publicity. Then, abandoning her social whirl for a stint of hard labour, she sailed for Vancouver, where Captain Nicholson and his crew loaded lumber aboard her to be taken to Kingcome for lay reader Ron Deane, Powell's replacement, to use in the building of a Sunday school. At Kingcome they continued their manual labour, transferring the lumber to boats, scows or canoes to be taken three miles upriver to the Indian village.

On her return trip, the *Columbia* towed the *Alan Greene* down to Vancouver to have her main engine repaired. She was turned over then to Archdeacon Ellis for patrol in the Cortes Island area, skippered by Don Maclean of Whaletown. The *John Antle* went briefly to Ron Deane at Kingcome. Don Maclean had come to the mission as a temporary lay reader in response to an appeal from Archdeacon Pat Ellis to help out when no clergymen were available. The crisis continued, and Maclean was with them almost a decade.

Ellis was preoccupied mainly with supervisory duties and trips to the east on mission business but, despite a heart attack shortly after joining the mission, he found time to tour his districts. It says much for his dedication that he willingly relinquished a comfortable parish to undertake many tasks incompatible with his health and personality.

In December 1962 he sailed in the *Alan Greene* to Kingcome, skippered by Maclean who reported the trip in *The Log*. Their visit to Kingcome was no luxury cruise. At Kingcome Ellis jumped from the *Alan Greene* into a 28-foot dugout that was paddled up and tied to her. The narrow, one-foot-wide seats in the dugout were uncomfortably hard during the trip upriver. Fog hung over the water, and they used a flashlight to locate and avoid the many stumps and snags. The river was icy cold at that time of the year, and Ellis anticipated a wade in knee-deep water, but the deckhand from the *John Antle* was on hand to welcome them at the mission and carried the tall archdeacon piggyback to the shore. They met a group at the mission attending a retreat conducted by Bishop Gower, after which Ellis and Maclean braved stormy weather on a round of Christmas visits.

The archdeacon played Santa at the Surge Narrows school, using the outhouse as a dressing room as was usual when Santas had to appear miraculously in the one-room schools. He hid the suitcase containing his clothes behind a tree, in case some child felt the urge to use the outhouse. Later in the evening he slipped out to retrieve his suitcase and change out of his Santa suit. It was a pitch-black night and he stumbled blindly about in the dark from one tree to another, getting thoroughly soaked by the rain before at last he discovered his cache.

The archdeacon suffered a serious fall on the *Columbia* the next year during a rough trip from Seymour Inlet to Alert Bay. A 50-m.p.h. gale was blowing, and the buffeting of the waves rocked and jolted the ship, pouring water all through her and throwing Ellis across the wheelhouse, breaking several of his ribs. The conscientious administrator had elected to tour the northern area, not in the pleasant months of summer pleasure-boating, but during the rough weather braved by the mission boats on their emergency runs.

In his superintendent's report of 1962, Ellis said he felt the medical service had outlived its value and was now a luxury service brought by ship to settlers' doors. Emergency cases were usually flown out to hospitals. He considered the shortage of priests would continue, due to small salaries, lack of proper accommodation and the difficulty of procuring for the smaller boats dual-purpose chaplains with seafaring experience and a master's ticket. The *Columbia*, staffed with both a skipper and chaplain, would not have this last problem. Other discouraging factors were the withdrawal of the community chest's $5000 grant and the shift in population from the C.C.M. areas to the southern towns due to the decrease in logging and fishing.

Another meeting of a Special Committee was held May 13, 1963 in the Synod Office in Victoria, composed this time of Archbishop Sexton, Bishop Gower, Dean Whitlow, Archdeacons Ellis, Hendy, Forth, Wetney, Colonel Mitchell and Messrs. Goold, Antle, Creery and Kaye. Bishop Gower urged a reorganization of the coastal area, keeping the Columbia Coast Mission name for its appeal to donors, with an archdeacon to look after the area from Sechelt to Kingcome. Ellis again asked for abolition of the office of superintendent.

At this time the committee recommended keeping the *Columbia*, abolishing the superintendent's office, making the Diocese of New Westminster responsible for Kingcome and its related villages, and Texada and adjacent communities, and the Diocese of Columbia responsible for northeast Vancouver Island, Port McNeill, Beaver Cove, Cortes, Lasqueti and Sayward. The C.C.M. Board would continue to administer grants and appoint staff. It was also recommended that a series of chaplains be appointed to serve in rotation.

Ellis wrote to Archdeacon Forth who headed the committee, protesting the idea of a series of chaplains in rotation. This would make a personal relationship between chaplain and parishioner almost impossible, and he cited the Reverend Iain Baird, then with the mission, whose excellent, continuous service had such good results.

By 1964 St. Mary's Church and the old people's home at Pender Harbour had been transferred to the Diocese of New

Westminster for administration, a resident pastor replacing the itinerant marine service. The parish of Port McNeill, Port Hardy and Beaver Cove was created and taken out of the marine mission's itinerary, as was the Cortes and Quadra area. The board was working towards the formation of permanent parishes with resident priests, and toying with the idea of planes to serve the outlying northern areas.

3

There had been some dissatisfaction with the schedule of the *Columbia*'s tours. Discussion arose concerning the changing relationship between captain, chaplain and doctor. Cecil Fitzgerald explained to the board that in John Antle's day, Antle was both captain and chaplain and operated his ship on a set route between the hospitals. When Captain Godfrey was taken on, Antle spent more time in supervisory and campaign work, but Godfrey continued to follow Antle's schedule, taking one week from Alert Bay to Seymour Inlet and one week south to Cortes, stopping off at innumerable camps, float houses and cabins *en route*. Visits of doctor and chaplain were necessarily brief, unless, like Heber Greene, the chaplain left the boat and conducted his visits on foot. After Godfrey left the service, skippers who followed felt the northern schedule then in force was too arduous and ran the ship their own ways. The succession of new chaplains and doctors, unfamiliar with the route, usually yielded to the captain's whims, and found their own schedules were often ignored.

To allow chaplain and doctor to function satisfactorily, Fitzgerald recommended that the *Columbia*'s chaplain be the supervisor of the *Columbia*'s work, both medical and missionary, responsible only to the bishop. He should live on the boat and have authority over the ship's movements, except in decisions regarding safety. He should co-operate with the doctor, and the captain should thoroughly understand the situation.

While this was considered, the *Columbia*'s staffing problem grew more acute than ever. For one period she was left without a skipper, doctor or chaplain. Captain Nicholson left in 1964 after five years of service and was succeeded by various skippers, including an Indian skipper, William Dick, assisted by Willie Hawkins of Kingcome, and followed by Charles Dick also of Kingcome.

Emergency calls still came in for the *Columbia*. One was in November 1964 when she was heading from Alert Bay to Bull Harbour. Skipper William Dick sighted the MV *Kalamalka* aflame and drifting off Pultney Point, west of Malcolm Island. Her distress signal was answered at once. A call was put in to Alert Bay (since the *Kalamalka* had no radio), firefighting equipment was passed over to her, and the passengers taken aboard the *Columbia*. The fire was extinguished, and the MV *Gospack* and MV *Alert Bay* arrived in answer to the *Columbia*'s call and took the *Kalamalka* in tow. That same day an emergency call for immediate medical attention came from Shoal Harbour, and the *Columbia* altered her course at once to respond. Aircraft had been unable to fly due to heavy fog and the crew of the *Columbia* felt a certain triumph as their ship sped through the mist to answer the call.

Women doctors were no longer a novelty; several who served on the *Columbia* during the steady turnover were Dr. Molly Towell, Dr. Claire Onhauser, Dr. Joyce Davies and Dr. Monica Shaketown. Chaplains also came and went, the Reverend Baird leaving in 1965 and the Reverend D. Rogers and the Reverend W.B. Parry filling in briefly.

The fifth *John Antle* was put up for sale at $17,800 in 1964 and sold to Ralph A. Smith of West Vancouver. Smith asked to retain the ship's name, as his wife (daughter of Harvey Bowering of Newfoundland) had heard her father's stories of John Antle during his Newfoundland parish days. Antle had christened her cousin, Treffie Bursey Harmon of Newfoundland, and had been a familiar sight to the family as he travelled up and down the coast, selling Bibles to the fishermen. The earlier *John Antle* ships were never registered with a number, though unofficially they were known by successive numbers, as were the *Columbias*. Thus, after some deliberation, the committee decided Smith could register the ship as the *John Antle II*, retaining the name so long as no other *John Antle* was acquired by the mission. This accounts for confusion arising when a photograph appeared later in newspapers advertising the sale of *John Antle II*. As the marine mission was disbanded five years later, successive owners were able to retain the name.

Smith was delighted to find the old mission collection box still aboard, along with patchwork quilts composed of squares from old suits and coats, donated by the Women's Auxiliaries.

Rob C. Stewart was the next owner, and ran her in the 1970s registered under his firm's name of Wyldene Stewart Investments Ltd. On their pleasure cruises up the Inside Passage, the Stewarts, like the Smiths before them, found that almost everywhere they anchored, several persons would ask to come aboard to look over the boat on which in the past they had been christened or married or had talked over good times and bad with a friendly chaplain.

Before withdrawing marine service from Kingcome, the mission bought a catamaran for the use of the Kingcome missionary, the Reverend Eugene Diespecker, who succeeded Ron Deane. The little craft was christened *Che-kwa-la* after a waterfall on one of the reserves; it meant "flowing water." The name was appropriate as Bishop Gower discovered when he dedicated the *Che-kwa-la*. The Reverend Eric Powell acted as bishop's chaplain, substituting for Diespecker who was attending a conference. *The Log* reported: "Someone forgot to fit the plugs into the self bailer and as the Bishop and others stood in the stern, water poured in." The bishop wondered if they would get the *Che-kwa-la* dedicated before she sank.

The *Che-kwa-la* suffered a series of breakdowns and could not be used for visiting the island reserves, but she managed to accompany the *Columbia* and the *Alan Greene* in 1965 from Kingcome to Campbell River, carrying dancers from the Kingcome band who put on a show of Indian dances there on two successive nights. The performance was especially exciting for Diespecker who was asked to take part in the lengthy

Grouse Dance, wearing a traditional Indian mask. On the way home, stormy weather struck, and one of the *Che-kwa-la*'s outdrives split apart. The Indians were forced to travel very slowly on one engine, with Dan Willie and Jimmy Dawson using paddles to steer. Just before they reached Kingcome the sea grew too rough for paddling. They put down the engine on the other drive and crept home, arriving tired and shaken.

Halfway through Diespecker's four years at Kingcome, the worst flood in 28 years hit the area. The water almost reached the floors of the houses though they were set on pilings five to six feet high. The only casualty, however, was the Venerable R. Stuart Faulks of Powell River who came up by plane to see the damage. He slipped on the plane float and fell into the sea, but was retrieved, having suffered only a thorough soaking. Archdeacon Faulks, who was in charge of the area from Sechelt to Kingcome, always took an active interest in the northern area and familiarized himself with its problems through many personal visits.

Archdeacon Ellis had collected material for a pictorial 60th Jubilee edition of *The Log*, assisted by Iain Baird. It was published in 1965, and a few months later Ellis retired from the Columbia Coast Mission to return to parish work in Surrey. The office and headquarters of the superintendent were now abolished.

4

The position of supervising chaplain of the *Columbia* was created, and filled by the Reverend Ivan Futter. It is possible that in Futter the board might have found an experienced chaplain with a master's ticket who would be willing to stay with marine mission work, but unfortunately he came into the organization at a time when the marine service was drawing to a close. The board was leaning increasingly towards the establishment of permanent parishes, resident priests and plane service in the north.

Futter, a stocky, red-bearded, soft-spoken sailor from Norfolk, England, had spent 12 years as navigating officer with the British merchant navy and then acted as second officer with the Canadian Pacific Steamship Company on the *Empress of Britain*. With these ships he had sailed both the east and west coasts of Canada, before settling down to run a pub called The Ship in the sailing port of Maldon in Essex. He had always wished to enter the church but had been advised in his student days to see more of the world before choosing his vocation.

His experience as a pub keeper, an item seized upon avidly by interviewers as an unusual prelude to priesthood, was presented as an asset when he applied to join the Columbia Coast Mission. He had already left his pub for study at the Theological College in Rochester, Kent, was admitted to priesthood in 1965 and was serving a two-year curacy in England. When he heard of the mission he believed his background was tailored to suit the work. He had the deep-sea experience, his pub days had taught him to relate to people, and his wife had adjusted to a life with a sailor husband often absent at sea. His application was accepted, a substitute was found to complete his term as curate, and the family emigrated to Canada in 1966, spending the first year in Campbell River.

Don Maclean acted as Honourary Lay Reader under Futter's direction for Cortes Island's three churches until December 1966. The following year Futter and his family moved to Port Hardy, and the *Columbia* made this port her base. The reason given for the choice of Port Hardy over more sheltered Port McNeill or Alert Bay was that rapid development was anticipated for Port Hardy, especially after the expected extension of the highway to that point. However, it was a poor choice for the *Columbia*'s home base. The narrow little bay where she anchored looked calm enough, with sailboats and canoes dotted on its waters, but to get down to Alert Bay it was necessary to come out around Dillon Point into the open waters of Queen Charlotte Strait where storms swept down from the sound.

There was an effort to make the ship's library a vital part of the service, as Antle had intended, by co-operation with the Vancouver Public Library. Then Futter set about the difficult task of relating to his varied parishioners while still maintaining their respect for the *Columbia* and its spiritual work. Whether or not it was due to his period of pub keeping, he possessed an easy, receptive personality that appeared to win him acceptance from both Indians and loggers. He credits his Indian captain, Charlie Dick, with helping him to understand Indian ways and avoid the pitfalls that prevented many whites from achieving a rapport with the natives. He had been told that a minimum of two years was needed before Indians would decide whether or not to accept him and confide in him, but with Charlie Dick leading the way, he felt he reached the point of acceptance long before two years had elapsed.

This was his first contact with Canadian Indians and there was much to learn. He was asked to conduct an Indian funeral and took the body and numerous relatives and friends on the *Columbia* from Alert Bay to Gilford Island. The body was taken to the longhouse and speeches began, and carried on, and on. Day faded into night as Futter waited patiently for his own service to be requested. Finally he was told, "Better go home now and come back tomorrow." It seems there was always a full day of speeches before the commitment on the second day.

It was not all smooth sailing. Numerous sects were eager to win over the natives to their particular creed. The Pentecostals made a habit of calling at the reserves a few hours in advance of a scheduled Anglican service. The *Columbia* would arrive to find the Indians engrossed in the rival service or dispersed to their homes with no stomachs for another sermon. Finally the chaplain told one particular village he was bypassing it unless requested to come, and for some weeks always sailed past the island on his tour. Then the chief came to Alert Bay where the *Columbia* was anchored and asked Futter to go to his island to help one of the young men who was ill.

Futter got to the island to find the whole village half berserk, in the throes of a wild drinking party, with men fighting up and down the street. Charlie Dick advised the chaplain not to go ashore; the Indian assistant flatly refused to go, but Futter decided he must keep his promise. Dick went with him, prophesying disaster, but beyond a few drunken catcalls they were unharmed, and brought out the violently delirious man, strapped to a stretcher, to the *Columbia* and on to Queen's Hospital. After that the temporary estrangement was healed and the *Columbia* resumed her calls.

If anyone could relate to the average itinerant logger it was surely a pub keeper, certainly one with understanding and a sense of humour. Futter called at a logging camp for the first time and walked into a big drinking party that was in progress. Empty bottles littered the floor and only one full bottle remained, standing upright on the table.

Taken aback by the unexpected appearance of the chaplain, one logger muttered sheepishly, "We're having a little party."

"Ah, but don't you know that's an evil thing?" demanded Futter reprovingly, pointing to the bottle. "... So let's kill it!" he ended cheerfully, and joined them in one last drink all round.

He was impressed by the welcome he received from those in solitary cabins or tiny settlements. Misunderstandings or resentments sometimes arose among the men or women, and Futter, with the *Columbia* tied up overnight, would hear their complaints, offer advice, and during a social hour aboard the vessel would usually see antagonism fade and harmony reign. From his retirement, Alan Greene told the mission board he considered Futter a real chaplain to the people of the coast because he understood them, and the *Synod Journal* reported him "an indefatigable worker and most conscientious in trying to serve the whole area."

Luckily the third *Columbia* was a sturdy ship, for her trips through Queen Charlotte Sound were severe tests. In 1960 she was running off tiny Pine Island in the sound when Hurricane Freda hit. All the windows in her wheelhouse were smashed before she got to shelter. Again in 1966 she was caught in a gale that blew her dinghy off the deck. The next moment a huge wave tossed it back on board again.

With a good ship like the *Columbia*, rough seas failed to

intimidate Futter. However, during a storm of hurricane strength, a great 50-foot wave struck little Pine Island, crushing the powerhouse and bending the radio beacon to a 35° list. The *Columbia* came by and anchored while Futter rowed to the island to inspect the damage. Fortunately, the family was unhurt as lighthouse keeper Rex Brown, his wife and two children had been asleep in their house when the wave struck. The house was only a few feet from the powerhouse but was undamaged. On Futter's return trip from his inspection, a wave washed over the dinghy and filled and sank it. Futter was wearing a life belt, but he nearly perished in the icy water as he struggled through the whitecapped swells to reach the *Columbia*.

Dr. F. Wiegand from Montréal had offered his services to the *Columbia* and paid his own fare to Hardy Bay to help to alleviate the doctor shortage. He also served the Whaletown clinic, and compiled a careful report on the medical work of the mission. In November 1966, he wrote that population was noticeably decreasing in the *Columbia*'s area, down to about 475. Kingcome's population was 75 compared to 250 three years previously. Here again, the closing of logging camps had resulted in a population shift to Campbell River, Nanaimo and other southern centres. Indians, Wiegand said, preferred to fly patients to St. George's Hospital rather than call for the ship.[2] Dr. Pickup of the hospital gave his opinion that the medical mission had outlived itself.

5

Now the end was in sight. The *Alan Greene* was sold for $10,475 in February 1967 to Stan Carnell who renamed her the *Montserrado*. The following year the *Columbia* was put up for sale. Planes had finally superseded the brave little ship. They could reach any port in the *Columbia*'s area within minutes, and there were as many as three regular flights a week to some of her ports of call. Futter had flown to his parishioners occasionally in the United Church plane with the pilot, the Reverend Newberry, and Newberry at other times accompanied Futter on the *Columbia*, but Futter was convinced that brief calls by plane were insufficient to establish the friendship and familiarity possible through more frequent, protracted visits by boat.

On her final run to Vancouver, with the Reverend Ivan Futter aboard and Captain Charlie Dick as skipper, the *Columbia* started off from Hardy Bay on December 2 into very rough seas. She battled wild seas all the way but she kept on going, though bigger vessels were running for shelter. She stopped in at Half Moon Bay overnight so Alan Greene could see her for one last time. Around five a.m. the waves were banging the ship so hard against the wharf that the crew had to let her go and steam around in the bay until seven a.m., when they continued on to Vancouver.

Futter said of the trip, "The seas were just fantastic and no matter which way you turned they seemed to come from every direction at once. But the *Columbia* rode each one proudly and bravely and never once shipped green water over her bow! She rolled, she pitched, she tossed, everything that could move on board, moved! But still she came up for more!"[3]

"When we say the *Columbia* is coming, she comes!" said Futter. It was the ship's unofficial motto, the slogan that showed one essential difference between ship and plane service.

The *Columbia* was sold for $37,000 to Mr. Jack Cash of Jack Cash Boat Charter, West Vancouver. It was considered a fair price since she was in need of a major overhaul. Her new owners added N to her name, making her the *Columbian*. Her chapel was transformed into staterooms and her surgery became the main lounge and dining room. A recent news article says she can still ride the storms at sea and bring her owners safely to port.

One final *Columbia* was to figure briefly in the history of the marine fleet, postponing the inevitable end of the service. Dr. M.E. Howe of North Vancouver offered the mission, through the Reverend Futter, a 42-foot pleasure yacht, the

Avolente, built in 1952 and operable by one man. A provision of the donation was that $10,000 should be spent in equipping her with radar, radio-telephone and echo sounder. Futter passed the offer on to the board, which decided to accept her. A stove, refrigerator, heat and radar equipment were installed and Futter agreed to run her during the summer and fall to see what repairs were needed. The plates had been removed from the third *Columbia* and these were placed on the fourth *Columbia* for her dedication on June 17, 1968, by Archbishop Gower.

Enthusiasm over the generous gift gave way to disillusionment. As a fine-weather ship she was adequate, but her quarters were crowded, with chaplain and deckhand required to share a cabin and clothes locker. Futter found the ship could make 11½ knots, but her engines were unreliable and with her shallow bottom and bluff bow she was considered unsuitable for use in rough northern waters. If the boats were still covering the southern area, the requirements might not have been so exacting. "A fine pleasure yacht but a disaster as a mission ship in the north," said Archbishop Gower. A pleasure boat could limit her sailing to fine weather days, but the mission ships were on call "anywhere, anytime."

Port Hardy was no place for her. In December she was stormbound and the chaplain had Christmas calls to make. On the morning of Christmas Eve the sea was still rough but the sky was clear and sunny, so he chartered a seaplane to take him to Gilford Island to hold a service. Futter found the village in an uproar as a young man was reported missing on a trip to Alert Bay. He had heard that his children had come up for the holidays from residential school and were at Alert Bay. Despite warnings from older people in the village that bad weather was brewing, he had set out in a small boat, eager to see his family. That was three days previously and no word had come from him since. Boats were searching the surrounding islands, but little hope was held for him as a gale had been blowing for the three days.

Abandoning plans for a sermon, Futter and the pilot climbed aboard the plane again and searched the area for two hours, finally abandoning hope and heading back for Port Hardy. Suddenly, far below them on the ocean, Futter caught sight of a tiny black speck. He pointed it out to the pilot, who banked steeply for a closer look. Sure enough, it was the lost man, rowing slowly and mechanically. They circled him, then flew to the nearest boat to leave directions and called Alert Bay Radio Station to send the Air Sea Rescue plane. They continued to circle the little rowboat until help arrived and took the man to his home. He had been blown by the storm into the shelter of a small island in Queen Charlotte Strait and stayed there for three cold days and nights without food or shelter, not daring to sleep lest he succumb to the cold. Said Futter, "For me, it was the best Christmas present that I have had for many years, to be instrumental in returning a father to his family."

At one point Futter declared he would not take the *Columbia IV* to sea again under any circumstances, but later agreed to run her if a replacement was found in the near future. Another purchase was considered, but by July 1969 it was decided to put the fourth *Columbia* up for sale. This final ship, so briefly a part of the fleet, was the only one bearing a number on her hull: *Columbia IV.*

On her trip down her engines failed. She went through Seymour Narrows on one engine and just as she was being docked her last engine cut and refused to start up again. The thought of drifting uncontrolled through the rapids was chilling to a mariner. The rakish little pleasure boat had come south to her proper sphere in the nick of time. In quieter waters she functioned well. R. Douglas of R. Douglas Agencies bought her, renamed her *Mahalo Nui II* and expressed himself as delighted with her performance.

So the last ship was sold, and the Columbia Coast Mission disbanded its marine service in 1969. Ivan Futter was called to a parish in North Saanich. The Venerable J. W. Forth having retired in this year, the Venerable R.S. Faulks was appointed acting superintendent until the new bishop was elected and made president of the mission board.

The archdeacon was asked to report on relative costs of

plane use. For some years the mission co-operated with the United Church in a plane service to isolated areas with its base at Nimpkish Lake on northern Vancouver Island. Bill Eliason, a retired R.C.A.F. pilot and United Church lay preacher, joined forces with Archdeacon John Mellis, the Anglican priest, who also had a pilot's licence. Together they visited camps, isolated homes and small communities in a Cessna 180. Scheduling calls proved awkward with one plane, and in 1978 the Columbia Coast Mission acquired its own matching Cessna. The board debated on a name, considering *John Antle,* but eventually deciding on *Columbia V.*

It was a whole new type of service, emphasizing speed. Planes came swiftly, but their stay was usually brief. Unless accommodation was offered, overnight visits were out. The plane was usually greeted with pleasure by dwellers in remote areas, but there was not the feeling of independence, of the opportunity to extend hospitality on board the mission boat instead of imposing on camps or homes. Lighthouses were no longer contacted. Plane landings were impossible in the wild waters surrounding the rocky northern islands. Ships stayed over, waiting for slack tides; their pace was more leisurely, their schedules elastic. Fog or storm seldom deterred them, whereas the flying chaplains admit they are fair weather flyers, usually back at the Nimpkish Lake base by dusk. They have, they say, a healthy respect for the area's strong wind patterns.

Still, the flying service is adapted to present conditions. The chaplains sometimes cover northern Vancouver Island by car and establish Bible classes, perform weddings and baptism services and fill the need for churches where no established church is within reach. The tradition of social gatherings for scattered dwellers is carried on whenever possible.

The passing of the ships was mourned by many. Archbishop Gower, who had been closely connected with the marine mission, had always believed with John Antle that separating the medical and spiritual work would be fatal. However, without sufficient funds to ensure permanent, steady support, the costly medical side could not be continued.

In 1966 the inadequate provision of dental services had been discussed by the mission, and a survey was made by the Provincial Dental Services to see if co-operation with the mission would ensure that more isolated areas not covered by the government were given dental care. As far back as 1957, Dr. Mary Woods had stressed the need for dental care. The Reverend Futter suggested this service when the marine fleet was being disbanded. He felt strongly that a small ship carrying a nurse and dentist and chaplain would fill a great need and retain the personal communication only possible with the ships. His suggestion was not acted upon by the board but shortly afterwards the Jehovah's Witnesses took up the idea with considerable success.

Eric Powell is another who regrets the loss of ships that stayed in port for days and allowed familiarity and friendship to develop between priest and parishioner. He says he was able to solve the problem of adolescent boys whose conduct had created difficulties by taking them aboard the *Alan Greene* as crew members. The work appealed to the young men and often the end of a cruise meant the end of a problem.

Antle's inspired dream of supplying the urgent needs of the north had been realized, but the mission fleet's part in the great work was over. The new era had substituted plane service for emergencies, and air and sea rescue service was available through the Coast Guard's Search and Rescue Department. The era had seen the start of camps with modern logging methods employing fewer loggers; these replaced the small camps dotting the route maps of the mission in its early days, and the resultant decrease in employment meant an exodus to the south. For the latter half of its history, the mission ships had ministered mainly to the spiritual and social needs of the people, yet the value of this service, less easily calculable, was of considerable worth in restoring or maintaining the mental health of the isolated settlers and inspiring them to continue the harsh, demanding work of opening up new areas and contributing to the growth of the province.

The missionaries of many denominations have affirmed, like Antle, that the church should "render service as well as hold services", and consider service an integral part of their religion. Antle was unique in his conviction that Christian service meant filling the crying need for hospital and social care with no "strings" attached; to offer but never pressure acceptance of the teachings of the church in which he himself was a firm believer; to give service even when services were rejected.

Generations of settlers in all walks of life up and down the British Columbia coast will remember the staunch little ships that fought their way through dense fog, wild rapids and stormy seas. The ships came to small, rockbound islands and travelled up the long, beautiful inlets, bringing laughter and companionship, consolation and spiritual inspiration to camps and settlements, and to men and women struggling against privation and loneliness in log cabins hidden in the forest wilderness.

The fleet took pride in keeping to its schedules despite stormy weather, often braving tide rips rather than waiting for slack water when distress calls signalled an emergency. Many of the skippers of the smaller ships came to the mission untrained in navigation and unfamiliar with west coast hazards, yet they plunged valiantly into the work, learning through experience as they went along. Perhaps the verses from "Psalms" read at the christening of the second *Columbia* sustained them as they sailed on missions of mercy through those perilous waters: "For he maketh the storm to cease, so that the waves thereof are still. Then are they glad because they are at rest, and so he bringeth them unto the haven where they would be."[4]

Columbia Coast Mission Ships

Alan Greene (Reg. #312802). Motor screw. Gross tonnage 13. Diesel engine, F. Perkins, Peterborough, Eng. 1 NHP. H.P. 65. Speed 8 knots. 33.3 x 10.0 x 6.0 feet (35 feet overall length.) Built 1959, Bissett's Boatbuilding Yards, North Vancouver, for Columbia Coast Mission. Sold 1967 to Stan Carnell. New name: *Montserrado*. Reg. trans. to Port of Victoria 1967.

Che-kwa-la. Catamaran donated 1964 by Columbia Coast Mission for use of Kingcome Mission.

Columbia (1) (Reg. #117017). Wooden yacht, motor vessel, gasoline screw, gross tonnage 38. 60.0 x 14.0 x 4.0 feet. First engine: 20 H.P. Union, replaced 1906, Standard Motor Construction Co. H.P. 4 sc. Ship built 1905 by Wallace Shipyards, Vancouver, for Columbia Coast Mission. Sold 1910, reregistered as *Chaos*. Material alterations in 1918 for Lockeport Canning Co., Ltd. Reg. owners in 1925: Frank Cvitanovich and Jack Fiomengo, Vancouver.

Columbia (2) (Reg. #126899) Wooden motor screw launch. Gross tonnage 106. 86.6 x 16.4 x 7.1 feet. (100 feet overall length). First Diesel engine replaced by 140 H.P. Atlas Imperial Diesel engine. Ship built 1910 by Dawe's Shipyard, New Westminster. Sold 1957, name reregistered as *Wayward Lady*, charter yacht, based in the Fraser River. Renamed *Lady Valentine* in 1958 and used as pleasure craft by owner Eric Griffiths of White Rock. Lost by fire in Annacis Slough in 1976.

Columbia (3) (Reg. #189231). Wooden yacht. Motor screw. Gross tonnage 73. 66.5 x 16 x 8.0 feet. H.P. 4 NHP. Diesel engine 1956 L. Gardner & Sons, Ltd. Speed 9 knots. Built 1956 by Star Shipyards, New Westminster for Columbia Coast Mission. Sold 1968 to Jack Cash Boat Charter, name reregistered as *Columbian*.

Columbia IV (Reg. #195443). Wooden yacht. Gross tonnage 24. H.P. 230 sc. Built 1952, Pender Island. Former name *Avolente*. 41.1 x 12.4 x 5.3 feet. Given to Columbia Coast Mission by owner Dr. M.E. Howe in 1968. Sold to R. Douglas in 1969, renamed *Mahalo Nui II*. Later owned by Victoria Importing and Exporting Co. of Victoria.

Eirene. Wooden launch. 30 feet. 10 H.P. engine. Loaned by owner J.C. Keith for summers of 1911 and 1912 to Columbia Coast Mission for use of student missionary Alan Greene.

Fredna. (Reg. #131143). Motor vessel. Gas screw engine, Scripps Motor Co., Detroit. Gross tonnage 5.96. H.P. lsc. 29.3 x 7.5 x 3.8 feet. Built 1912 by W.R. Menchions, Vancouver, for E.E. & F.W. Cunningham. Loaned to Columbia Coast Mission in 1930 by owner Francis H.M. Codville, Egmont, B.C. Sold to James Dick, Cumberland, Nov. 28, 1934. Owned in 1945 by Bloedel Stewart and Welch Ltd. Vessel sank in Great Central Lake, B.C. in 1949. Total loss.

Governor Musgrave. Lady Musgrave donated this small mission launch, named in 1911 after her husband, Sir Anthony Musgrave, governor of the Crown Colony of British Columbia from 1869 to 1871. The Reverend Fred Comley ran her when a lay missionary at Van Anda (1914–19) and Alert Bay (1925–28).

Gwa-Yee. Small launch, former name *Bob*, donated by C.C.M. for use of Kingcome mission, 1945. Replaced by yacht *Veracity*, owner E. Christmas.

John Antle (1). (Reg. #153731). Wooden yacht, copper bottomed & rivetted, double teak planking. Gross tonnage 67. H.P. 5 sc. 74.2 x 13.2 x 9.7 feet. (75 feet overall length). Built 1921 by Thornycrofts, Hampton-on-Thames, Eng. Former name: *Syrene*. Donated 1933 to C.C.M. by B.C. and Yukon Church Aid Society, England. Sold 1936 to Harry R. Rendell, Vancouver. New name: *Syrene I.* Reg. 1938 to Charles H. Kennedy; 1939 to Wm. C. Mainwaring; 1942 to Minister of Lands, Victoria; 1980 to Harry R. Rendell.

John Antle (2) (Reg. #153313). Motor vessel. Gross tonnage 28. H.P. 3½sc. 55.0 x 14.5 x 6.0 feet (overall length 60 feet). Built 1926 at Houghton, Wash. for Nitinat Packers Ltd. Reg. 1927 to Seymour Navigation Co., Van., then to B.C. Packers. Original name: *Florida V.* Sold to Columbia Coast Mission in 1936 and renamed *John Antle*. Sold 1945 to Ranta, Salo and Ranta, tuna fishermen, Port Angeles.

John Antle (3) (Reg. #171809) Motor vessel. Gross tonnage 17. Gas engine, 1939, Gray Marine Motor Co., Detroit. NHP 1. Speed 7 knots. 25 x 7.5 x 5.4 feet. Built 1932 Vancouver Shipyards for Arthur Falkland and Howard Head, Cobble Hill. Original name: *Panda*. Sold to Columbia Coast Mission 1945, redesigned by Gilbert Jukes, Van. Shipyards. New dimensions 1945: 25.7 x 10.6 x 5.3 feet. New name: *John Antle*. In 1956 name changed to *Laverock II*. Given in 1957 to Anglican Synod of the Diocese of Caledonia by Columbia Coast Mission.

John Antle (4) (Reg. #172382) Wood yacht. Gross tonnage 19. H.P. 165. 44.0 x 11.0 x 4.7 feet. Built 1940 Edward Wahl's Shipyard, Prince Rupert. Former name: *Western Hope,* owner Anglican Diocese of Caledonia. Rebuilt by them in 1947 in Prince Rupert. Donated to Columbia Coast Mission 1953, named changed to *John Antle*. Renamed 1957 *Rendezvous*. (Overall length 1957 given as 45 feet). Sold 1962 to Great Northwest Charter Lines, N. Van. Later owned by Rendezvous Dive Ventures Ltd., Port Alberni, name *Rendezvous* retained.

John Antle (5) (Reg. #198078). Wood yacht. Motor screw. Gross tonnage 9.03. Diesel engine 1956 General Motors Corp., Detroit. NHP 2. Speed 9 knots. 43.8 x 13.2 x 8 feet. Built 1956 Star Shipyards, New Westminster, for Columbia Coast Mission. Sold 1964, name changed to *John Antle II*. Reg. to Ralph A. Smith, International Factory Sales Service Ltd. Reg. 1974 to Rob C. Stewart, Wyldene Stewart Investments Ltd., Van., name *John Antle II*. Name changed to *John Antle* 1977, reg. to 1647 Investments Ltd., Van. Boat and company sold 1978, reg. under 1647 Investments Ltd. Frequently seen berthed in Nanaimo.

Laverock II (Reg. #171809) See *John Antle* (3) (Reg. #171809)

Makehewi (Reg. #131150) Wood launch, motor vessel. Gross tonnage 13.7. H.P. 1 ⅘ sc. Union Gas Engine Co., San Francisco. 35.1 x 11.2 x 4.0 feet. Built 1910, foreign name: *Charlotte S.* Rebuilt Port Blakeley, Wash. name changed to *Makehewi* by owner Wm. Sulley, Jr., Van., 1912. Sold to C.C.M. Oct. 6 1920, reg. Jan. 13, 1921. Sold 1924 to Bertram O. Pender, lumberman, Van. Sold 1927 to Thomas Campbell, boatbuilder. Sold 1931 to Alvin S. Miller, Roberts Creek. Registry closed 1935.

Rendezvous (1) (Reg. #151177). Wood launch, motor vessel. Gross tonnage 12. 4 cyl. gas engine 1924 Kermath Motor Co., Detroit. Speed 7½ knots. 31.3 x 10.0 x 4.7 feet. Built 1924 Hoffar Motor Boat Co., Van. for Columbia Coast Mission. Sold 1955 to Edward C. Tooker. Rereg. 1956 as *Tari Jacque*. Still used 1980 for summer fisheries patrol work.

Rendezvous (2) (Reg. #172382) See *John Antle* (4) (Reg. #172382)

Footnotes

Chapter One: Beginnings

1 Cecil Fitzgerald tells this story. Alan Greene, retelling it years later, says John Glassford was a grandson of George Gibson after whom Gibson's Landing was named.

2 The Methodists established a hospital in Fort Simpson in 1891 and in Bella Bella in 1898. For a time they also ran a hospital in Rivers Inlet in the summer during the fishing season. North of Bella Bella, the Anglican Bishop Perrin in the 1890s appointed a qualified medical missionary, the Rev. A.H. Sheldon, to Port Essington. Sheldon was lost at sea in an Indian canoe *en route* to Port Simpson. Still farther north was Metlakatla, an Anglican medical mission in the early 1890s, under Dr. Vernon Ardagh.

3 *The Log*, July-August 1949.

4 Antle, John: Memoirs

5 Ibid.

6 Ibid.

7 Ibid.

8 British Columbia was divided into three dioceses in 1879: British Columbia (or Columbia), covering Vancouver Island and adjacent islands; New Westminster, covering the lower mainland; and Caledonia in the north. In 1914 the Church Province of British Columbia was formed and Bishop Du Vernet was elected Archbishop of Caledonia and Metropolitan of British Columbia (all B.C.) The Bishop of British Co-

lumbia (or Columbia) retained the diocese of British Columbia (Vancouver Is. and adjacent islands.) The chairman of the C.C.M was later titled president.

9   *The Log*, May 1906

10 *The Log*, April 1906

11 from the first Report to the Joint Committee of the Dioceses of Columbia and New Westminster, Jan. 3, 1906, by Rev. J. Antle

12 Letter from Mrs. Meg Shaw to the author, dated Nov. 14, 1980.

13 Charles Forrest, (son of J. McKelvie Forrest, postmaster and storekeeper at Shoal Bay from 1899 to 1915) writes that his sister was the first white child born in Queen's Hospital, the original hospital at Rock Bay. Another sister was born in Columbia Hospital on Texada Island.

Chapter Two: The Fleet Expands

1   from a letter to the author from Capt. W.G. Dolmage of Halfmoon Bay, brother-in-law of Dan McGregor, dated Jan. 14, 1981.

2   extract from a letter to the editor in *The Log*, Sept.-Oct. 1945.

3   Johnston, Lukin, *Beyond the Rockies* (London, Dent, 1929).

4   *The Log*, June 1930

5   *The Log*, Nov. 1930

Chapter Three: To The Rescue in Depression Days

1   Letter from D.D., Saskatoon, Sask; in *The Log*, November 1933

2   *The Log*, August 1931

3   *The Log*, June/July 1931

4   Report of the Superintendent of the C.C.M. for the year ending December 31, 1936

5   from a letter from Dr. Keith Whittaker to the author, dated May 13, 1981

6   *The Log*, Mar.-May 1936

7   Honor Kidd: "John Antle". Article in the *Canadian Medical Association Journal*, 1951

Footnotes

8   Robson Black: "The Skipper of the Columbia," Article in *The American Magazine*, reprinted in *The Log*, June 1930
9   Grove, Lyndon: *Pacific Pilgrims* 1979
10 *Daily Province* Sept. 27, 1940. Interview with Antle
11 Ibid.

Chapter Four: New Priorities: The War Years

1   C.C.M. Superintendent's Annual Report, 1938.
2   Letter from Douglas Dane, headed "Ballenas Island Light Station," to Alan Greene in *The Log* Jan/Feb 1937
3   letter to the author from Mrs. Elmer Ellingsen, dated Oct. 25, 1980
4   *The Log,* Nov.-Dec. 1946
5   letter from Mrs. Ellingsen, 1980
6   interview with the author, 1980
7   from a letter to the author from Mrs. Bertha Reedel, dated Nov. 10, 1980. Mrs. Reedel's brother, Ed Tooker, bought the first *Rendezvous* from the mission and still runs it, as the *Tari Jacque*. Our Lady of Lourdes Hospital, referred to by Mrs. Reedel, was the original name of Campbell River's hospital.
8   from a newspaper profile in the possession of Mr. John T. Bayfield of West Vancouver. Author, date and source unknown.
9   *Daily Colonist*, Nov. 13, 1932. "Messengers of Mercy on B.C. Coast", by Colonel H.T. Goodland, C.B., D.S.O.
10 *The Log,* Nov.-Dec., 1946
11 *The Log*, Sept.-Oct. 1944
12 *The Log*, Nov.-Dec. 1944
13 *The Log*, Jan.-Feb. 1946
14 John Antle, Memoirs, p. 42

Chapter Five: Changing Times and Needs

1   Greene, Alan, *Scattered Sheep*, 1920 (pam)
2   *The Log*, Jan.-Feb. 1946
3   C.C.M. Superintendent's Report, 1950

4 interview with the author, 1980

5 Student Anthony is now the Rev. T.M. Anthony, B.A. (U.B.C.), S.T.M., director, National and World Program, Anglican Church of Canada

6 Bishop Gower became the Most Reverend Godfrey Gower, Archbishop of New Westminster and Metropolitan of B.C. in 1968.

7 from the hymn *Father, Hear the Prayer* (*Gott des Himmels*) by Love Maria Willis, 1824–1908, and others. Adapted by Charles Steggal (1826–1905) from melody by Heinrich Albert (1604–1651)

8 *Vancouver Sun*, Jan. 5, 1960. Article by Jean Howarth

9 Alan Greene's first wife Gertrude died in 1960. He married his second wife, Dorothy Andrews, in England in 1962.

Chapter Six: The Last Years

1 letter of Ernest S. Antle to Rev. P.R. Ellis July 24, 1961.

2 Dr. Frederick M. Wiegand's Report on the Medical Phase of the Mission. November 1966.

3 *The Log*, Easter 1968

4 Anglican Church, *Book of Common Prayer*, Psalm 107, verses 29, 30

Sources

Books

Carrington, Philip, *The Anglican Church in Canada.* Toronto, Collins, 1963.

Craven, M., *I Heard the Owl Call My Name.* Toronto, Clarke, 1967.

———, *Again Calls the Owl.* New York, Putnam, 1980.

Cronin, Kay, *Cross in the Wilderness.* Vancouver, Mitchell Press, 1960.

Grove, Lyndon, *Pacific Pilgrims.* 1979.

Molson, K.M., *Pioneering in Canadian Air Transport.* James Richardson and Sons, 1974.

Morley, Alan, *Roar of the Breakers; a biography of Peter Kelly.* Toronto, Ryerson, 1967.

Peake, Frank A., *The Anglican Church in British Columbia.* Vancouver, Mitchell Press, 1959.

Johnston, Lukin, *Beyond the Rockies.* London, Dent, 1929.

Runnalls, F.E., *In God's Country, a review of the United Church and its sounding partners, the Congregational, Methodist and Presbyterian Churches in British Columbia.* Ocean Park, B.C., 1974.

Rushton, G.A., *Whistle Up the Inlet.* Vancouver, J.J. Douglas, 1974.

Wand, J.W.C., *Anglicanism in History and Today*. London, Weidenfeld and Nicolson, 1961.

Pamphlets

Greene, Alan, *Scattered Sheep,* n.d.
Columbia Coast Mission, *History*, n.d.
Anglican Church of Canada, *The Columbia Coast Mission,* n.d.

Magazines

Columbia Coast Mission, *The Log*, 1906–1909; New series 1930–1973.
Canadian Medical Association Journal, 1951, 64, 484–489, Kidd, Honor, "John Antle".

General Reference

Canada. Department of Transport. List of Shipping. Ottawa, 1905–1980.

Reports

Anglican Church of Canada, Columbia Coast Mission, *General Correspondence In and Out* 1939–1974.
Annual Reports 1936–1950.
Anglican Church of Canada, Diocese of British Columbia, *Synod Journals*.

Unpublished Material

Antle, John, *Memoirs* (typescript) n.d.
Cross, Robert George, *A Biographical Study of Canon Greene, D.D.,* 1973. (thesis, typescript)
Lonsdale, Richard, *History of the Columbia Coast Mission,* (thesis, typescript)
Powell, E.D., *B.C. Marine Missions,* 1958 (thesis, typescript)

Newspapers

The Colonist, Victoria
The Province, Vancouver
The Vancouver Sun
Westminster Daily News

Sources

Tapes

Speeches by Alan Greene, including brief history of the Columbia Coast Mission and anecdotes concerning mission work, in the possession of Alan F. Greene.

Interviews

Mr. Ernest Antle
Mr. and Mrs. John T. Bayfield
Mr. and Mrs. Chris Dalton
Archdeacon Patrick Ellis
Mr. Cecil Fitzgerald
The Reverend Ivan Futter
Archbishop Godfrey Gower
Mr. Alan F. Greene
Dr. Harvey Hamilton
Mr. Derek Lukin Johnston
Bishop Hywel Jones
Mrs. George MacDonald
Mr. Robert McCrea
Mr. Douglas Morton
The Reverend Eric Powell
Mr. Ralph A. Smith
Mrs. Rob Stewart
Mrs. Catherine Greene Tuck
The Reverend Cyril Venables
The Reverend Trefor Williams

Correspondence

Mrs. H.L. Bendickson
Captain W.G. Dolmage
Mrs. Elmer Ellingsen
Mr. Charles Forrest
Mrs. F. Mennis
Mrs. Bertha Reedel
Mrs. Meg Shaw
The Reverend and Mrs. Joseph Titus

Index